c 1786
998

P9-CJM-387

1786
998

TWENTY ROLLS-

PAINTINGS BY *Melbourne Brindle*

TEXT · PHIL MAY   INTRODUCTION · JULIEN LEVY

SILVER GHOSTS
ROYCE

THE INCOMPARABLE
PRE-WORLD WAR I MOTORCAR
1907 – 1914

DOUBLEDAY & COMPANY, INC.
GARDEN CITY, NEW YORK   1978

Paintings illustrations, by Melbourne Brindle.
Text by Phil May.

Originally published in 1971 by McGraw-Hill Book
Company, a subsidiary of McGraw-Hill, Inc.
This edition publishd in 1978 by Doubleday &
Company, Inc.

All rights reserved under Berne and Pan-American
Copyright Conventions.
Reproduction in whole or in part of any portion of the
text or any of the illustrations without permission
from the publisher is prohibited.

Produced and prepared by Chanticleer Press, Inc.,
New York

Library of Congress Catalog Card Number: 78-8806
ISBN: 0-385-14668-x

Printed in Italy

TABLE OF CONTENTS

HENRY ROYCE WROUGHT THE FINEST MOTORCARS IN THE WORLD.

ASSOCIATION WITH THEM BRINGS OUT THE FINEST IN A MAN.

IT ATTRACTS THE METICULOUS CRAFTSMAN AND LEADS HIM TO HIS

BEST THINKING AND TALENTS. IT WAS IN THIS SPIRIT THAT

I APPROACHED THE PAINTINGS OF THIS GROUP OF FINE AUTOMOBILES.

I WOULD HOPE THAT I HAVE DONE THEM JUSTICE.

MELBOURNE BRINDLE

INTRODUCTION

The occasion for a meeting of artist and technician within the compass of one man is rare and invaluable. In these days of specialization the right hand of the scientist seldom can understand what the left hand of the poet is doing. With this series of paintings, *Twenty Silver Ghosts*, Melbourne Brindle adds his name to the list of American "Magic Realists"* he has long admired: Audubon, Harnett, Sheeler, Andrew Wyeth. These paintings become more than a presentation, they become a celebration.

Does the spark that ignites inspiration come from the magneto of the mind or from the spirit? In these portraits of Rolls-Royce motor cars Brindle not only immortalizes a legend, he makes an impassioned demonstration of a union between fidelity and imagination, accuracy, and glamour. These paintings, in the artist's words, "represent the result of a fifty-year love affair."

"I was standing on a sidewalk, in 1919, in San Francisco. It was standing at the curb. Post Street, near the corner of Stockton," he tells us. "It was gray. The top was down. A uniformed chauffeur sat at the wheel. I looked the car over from where I stood, and he looked me over from where he sat. I stepped out in front to inspect the radiator and tremendous headlamps and bonnet. The bonnet was untapered, so it was pre-1913. Seemingly without a move from the chauffeur, the engine suddenly came to life, noiselessly, and without a starter. He had achieved this without getting out to crank the car, and this mystified me, as those were the days when you had to crank your automobile. It was years before I learned how he did it. I found out that if you had your spark control set just in a certain way, ready, and the piston of one of the six cylinders at its top, primed and ready, then just a fractional move of the ignition caught that spark, forced the piston down a step, suddenly, and spontaneously, it would seem, the engine would come to life.

"This was not quite the beginning of my 'affair.' Many years before I came to America I remember walking barefoot on the esplanade in Dromana, Australia. I remember being on the left side of the road. The car passed me on the off side and slightly below my level. It was silhouetted against the sea. It was a hot summer's day and the top was down. It seemed very low to the road, but perhaps that was because I was used to my family's horse-drawn phaeton. I believed it to be traveling at speed, although I suspect that was purely relative. It was heading for Melbourne, my namesake city, some 45 miles away at the head of Port Phillip Bay. Surely it had come from Sorrento 13 miles below us.

"The road surface was what we called 'metaled' and the car left a plume of dust in its silent passing. I turned to watch as it disappeared, leaving only the dust and a novel and rather heady smell of burnt petrol.

"Although I had no way of knowing at that moment that I had seen my first Rolls-Royce, the effect of this meeting on me was so sharply pleasurable it was to last a lifetime. So pleasurable that I, usually shy, talked about the brief encounter with others who had seen it also. One person said it was a Rolls-Royce belonging to a Mr. Solomon Green of Melbourne.

"I can clearly remember my boyhood vision of that car today. Just by closing my eyes I can bring the picture back. I think I could sketch it now in some detail.

"I could draw," he says, "almost as soon as I could draw breath. But as a boy, and on into my seventeenth year, my ambition was to become a chauffeur, always at the wheel of a Rolls-Royce, of course. I knew how to drive—here I had another talent. And I always felt that a truly well-designed automobile is an art form in itself, a more-than-worthy subject for a painting."

And so when Melbourne Brindle talks about the structure of an automobile he talks about the anatomy of art.

"She had a beautiful, clean radiator, bonnet and sweep of wings—we call them fenders. All the spark and throttle control rods had ball-and-socket joints, better than anything today. There was precise control of all the moving parts throughout to the millionth of an inch. . . . And those wooden wheels! In these days of pressed steel wheels and undistinguished wheel covers, those wheels are a joy to behold. The decision to allocate fourteen spokes to the rear wheels and only ten to the front, when the mode was twelve all round, was a happy one. The distinctive treatment of the wheel felloes was a stroke of pure genius!"

All through the 1920s Melbourne Brindle haunted the Rolls-Royce show-room on Post Street. He became a fixture at the Service Depot. He had to have a Rolls-Royce of his own, and couldn't possibly afford to buy one. So he began to build a synthetic one.

Three years later the car was ready for the road. It was a handsome convertible coupe, gray, with black Dunlop wire wheels. It was composed of parts from 11 different cars, but mainly from his own 1915 Model D Stevens-Duryea, built in Chicopee Falls, Massachusetts, and until then his favorite car. Rolls-Royce supplied the steering wheel, headlamps, bumpers, front fenders, and trunk rack. The "Early and Late" quadrant took quite a bit of doing. His brother made the radiator to the exact dimensions of the Rolls-Royce, all of German silver. He designed a radiator nameplate in the Rolls-Royce manner, substituting *BB*, for Brindle Brothers, in place of *RR*.

So Melbourne Brindle's romance did not remain at a distance. Like another Pygmalion he created his own Galatea. "And I had 'The Spirit of Ecstasy,' the Flying Lady, on the radiator front. This car had six forward speeds. I wish I had it back. It was left in my brother's care, demolished in an accident, and unfortunately sold for junk while I was out of town. This car was something I was permeated with, loved, and worked on with my hands in the grease—something a painter should never do, I am told—but much that was generated with it enables me to paint my pictures today.

"Through the years I have owned other interesting cars. Stevens-Duryea, Crane-Simplex, Locomobile, Rolls-Royce, Packard. But none commands my respect or stimulates my imagination as does Rolls-Royce, especially those of the golden era before World War I. And so, this book of paintings.

"Most painters avoid mechanical objects as subjects, although I don't know why. Mechanical things are very perishable, as opposed to objects of nature. Audubon, for example, painted pictures of American birds that are unsurpassed, even today. Yet, except perhaps for the passenger pigeon, most of the birds are still extant. James and John Bard, on the other hand, painted a priceless record of early paddlewheel steamboats for posterity. The boats are all gone now, but we have the paintings. There are few paintings of early automobiles. I am trying to remedy that.

"My first painting was the 1910 Barker flush-side torpedo. I saw the car when it was touring this country in 1957. It was like my first Rolls-Royce all over again. I couldn't wait to get back to my studio. I consider this Ghost one of the most beautiful ever built.

"These paintings have satisfied my love of detail. Everything must be right. If you'll count, you'll find there are exactly thirty-four round-headed rivets on either side of the three hinges on a Silver Ghost bonnet. There are sixteen sections in each of the three hinges. I know the radiator core is recessed three-quarters of an inch behind the front edge of a 1911 Ghost radiator. Eighty-six spokes make one wire wheel on the 1910 Barker torpedo."

Here are distillations of Melbourne Brindle's dedication, his deep feeling for form, for grace, for glowing detail, and for the same painstaking perfection that guided the genius of Mr. Royce himself.

The paintings are impressive additions to the *trompe l'œil* tradition (in America the tradition of Harnett, Péto, and Rembrandt Peale) with imaginative and even surrealist overtones in the choice of landscape and mementos, astonishing and convincing because of the artist's flawless control of his brush.

JULIEN LEVY
BRIDGEWATER, CONNECTICUT

---

* *Magic Realists*—a category invented for the title of an exhibition, "American Realists and Magic Realists," presented by the Museum of Modern Art, New York, 1943.

ABOUT THAT FASCINATING ERA— PRE—WORLD WAR I

THE EDWARDIAN ERA

Edward VII became sovereign of the British Empire at 6:30 P.M. on Tuesday, January 22, 1901. What was to come is perhaps best described by R. J. Minney in his book *The Edwardian Age* as, "... a frenzied, flamboyant assertion of freedom after the long, severe, puritanical restraints of the reign of Queen Victoria."

Frenzied, flamboyant, opulent, lavish, profuse, gay, magnificent, revolutionary—all are words that could apply to the Edwardian era. A few of them could be applied to the new King himself, because his personality closely paralleled the personality of England during the days of his reign.

Edward was sixty years old when he ascended the throne. His mother's reign had been the longest in English history. He had been groomed to be King since his birth, yet he often must have felt like a theatrical understudy waiting in the wings for a robust star to get ill. Rather than sit around and twiddle his thumbs during what was to be the longest heir-apparency, Edward decided early in life to enjoy himself, and his unique position, to the fullest.

Edward became a playboy. He traveled to all the right spots, with all the right people. He spent hours at cards. He had affairs with women, although only three of these became public scandals. He frequented race courses. He rode motorcars. He ate voraciously and looked it. He had gout.

Prince Albert had decided upon an intense educational life for his son. Governors were appointed to keep strict discipline in all the activities of the future King. Edward rebelled against it and looked for some form of release. Finally, after one of Edward's indiscretions, Prince Albert left a sickbed to visit his son in Cambridge. Worry and the journey aggravated his condition, and he died soon after.

The death of his father ended the grueling period of Edward's life. His mother blamed him for Albert's death and insisted that he travel so that he would be out of her sight. She also resolved to keep him out of affairs of state.

Edward married Princess Alexandra of Denmark on March 10, 1863. The young couple took up residence at Marlborough House in Pall Mall and enjoyed a honeymoon of balls and receptions that lasted for months and caused Queen Victoria much concern.

This is not the place to set down the entire life of Edward VII. Suffice it to say that he was the exact opposite of his mother; so it is not difficult to understand how stunned the country was when Queen Victoria was actually gone and Edward took the throne.

For one thing, Victoria was an institution. She had been Queen as long as most people alive could remember. She had given her name to a period in history. What would happen now that her royal but disreputable son was in charge?

King Edward took his new duties very seriously and brought into play many sides of his character that most people didn't know existed. For one thing, he was decisive, and proved it by letting the people know they had a sovereign again.

Queen Victoria had gone into isolation when Prince Albert died. In his suites, his clothes and medicines were put out daily as though he would return from the dead and use them. Royal castles looked like tombs and were not maintained well. The Queen was seldom seen in public places, and she wore black until the day she died. Edward, on the other hand, was a mover and a shaker, and he began to move things his way from his first day as King, shaking out all the dusty remnants of his mother's reign.

Edward's first name was Albert (his nephew, Kaiser Wilhelm II of Germany, called him Uncle Bertie), and his mother had always told him never to drop his father's name. She said he should be King Albert Edward I of England. On the day of her death the new King rode to London to take the oath. He announced to the Privy Councillors that he wished to be known by the name of Edward. Shortly after this, during Victoria's funeral, Edward was in the yacht *Victoria and Albert*, following the royal yacht bearing his mother's body. He noticed that the Royal Standard on his boat was flying at half mast. When he asked why, he was told that the Queen was dead. He answered that the King of England was alive, and ordered the standard raised to the top of the mast. That was just the beginning.

Edward liked the theatre; so the theatre became fashionable. He wore a beard; so more and more men grew beards. His top hat became *de rigueur* for men of means. Race meetings became social affairs. Dining took on a new importance.

Courtship always started at the dinner table. Restaurants frequented by the noble and wealthy had private rooms set aside for young couples in love. In most of these private rooms, a small settee was provided. After the dessert, and after the waiter had cleaned up and gone out, there was little doubt what went on. Still later, larger private rooms in restaurants were provided with beds that folded down from the wall. Some Edwardians were indeed a liberated group!

During the last few years of Victoria's reign, women had become more daring as a group. They quietly invaded several areas of business to become secretaries, waitresses, and telephone operators. A few became doctors, and some attempted to gain admittance to the law courts. Noblewomen joined the movement, opening shops and small companies. Then came the matter of votes for women.

Queen Victoria was adamant on the subject, calling it "mad wicked folly." Still, petitions were sent to Parliament each year, and denied each year. It all came to a head two years after Edward became King.

Women began disrupting the House of Commons by gaining admittance to the gallery and showering leaflets and banners on the M.P.s. It was hard to keep them out, as even the most meek-looking lady could turn into a tiger in the House. Finally the militant women began chaining themselves to the grilles which had been installed in the galleries to stop the leaflet throwing. Embarrassed policemen would have to remove the grilles before they could remove the women.

The King didn't approve of this kind of thing. He wanted women to stay the delightful and feminine creatures he enjoyed so much. That was just what the women were rebelling against.

Soon the suffragettes began to make such nuisances of themselves that the police began arresting them and giving harsh prison sentences. Still the ladies continued to make their presence felt at every large gathering. They made life very difficult for one young M.P. named Winston Churchill, including efforts to prevent him from taking his seat after he had been promoted to the Cabinet. Churchill, who had once been in favor of women's suffrage, admitted he was changing his mind.

The whole issue was not resolved until 1918, eight years after King Edward's death. Women over the age of thirty were permitted to vote and sit in Parliament.

Certainly not all the women in England had engaged in the suffrage movement. Most of the wealthy set were content to live the high life that seemed to consist mainly of weekend visits to country estates of "friends." The King was an active participant in these elaborate country jaunts.

Complicated was certainly one of the words that applied to these visits, since it usually meant that about fifty people invaded someone's estate beginning Friday afternoon and ending Monday afternoon. Keeping up with the social whirl could be a financial disaster for those within the circle whose means were not what they looked to be.

Most visitors would arrive by train and be met with a mixed assortment of carriages and motorcars to convey them to the house of the victim. Along with the people came mounds of baggage and servants to help the ladies dress. The men brought along their cased shotguns, riding clothes, and billiard cues.

Once the guests were firmly ensconced in their apartments, the first order of the day was to change clothes. Men usually changed their complete attire four times a day. The women often changed more times than that, and indeed, on looking back, some of the ladies admitted that a great deal of their time in the Edwardian era was spent getting in and out of clothes.

During these visits, men usually went off by themselves to take part in some sport or another. Ladies would take tea and sew, chatting all the while. Afternoons were often taken up with games of croquet, one of the King's favorite social pastimes.

The King did not take an active, personal, part in sport at the lower level (although he loved horses and hunting, and was one of the finest game shots in the country), but he showed a keen interest in many activities. The Royal Automobile Club and the Royal Aero Club were two which enjoyed the King's patronage.

While a more adventuresome and enlightened outlook was enjoyed during the Edwardian years within England, the country also benefited on the international level. Edward had been a traveler, both by the Queen's dictates and by choice, while he was Prince of Wales. He knew that England could not continue to remain apart from the alliances that were being formed on the Continent and around the world. Early in his reign he began to extend England's hand to other nations.

One ideal alliance might have been with King Edward's nephew, Kaiser Wilhelm II of Germany. The Kaiser had great admiration for England, but public sentiment within his country was anti-British; so nothing was done. Edward had to look elsewhere for his partners.

He looked to France, where relations had been quite cool because of numerous small incidents that almost brought the two countries to war. With a determination few knew he possessed, King Edward set out to woo France and accomplished his aim almost single-handedly. He visited Paris and was met with jeering crowds for the most part. But by the end of his visit the French were cheering him. The result of this visit was the famous Entente Cordiale. The Entente was not a military alliance; yet it paved the way for one later. In 1907, Edward journeyed to Russia to visit another nephew, Czar Nicholas II, and soon the Entente Cordiale became the Triple Entente with the inclusion of Russia. And so we see that the countries who were to go to war in 1914 aligned themselves during the reign of Edward VII.

The Edwardian era could perhaps be called the naïve period in twentieth-century living. It was a transitional period that saw the growth of industry into a gigantic institution. Social reform began to improve the plight of the working man. Motorcars, experimented with and refined during the Edwardian decade, changed many aspects of life. Aircraft were developed in the period. Wireless communication was refined. Moving pictures became a popular diversion for people in all walks of life. Electricity came into its own as the best means of lighting and powering homes and industries. Edward was not only a new King in a new century, he was seeing a new kind of world emerge.

To be precise, one could say that the Edwardian age ended at 11:45 on May 6, 1910. King Edward had been working very hard while still adhering to his heavy social calendar. He was sixty-eight years old and very tired. Bronchitis led to several heart attacks, and he died a few hours after congratulating the Prince of Wales on a race his horse had won.

In truth, the Edwardian period could be extended past the death of King Edward to the beginning of World War I. When England emerged from that conflict, the country had a new outlook and had caught up with itself. The Edwardian era was over, but it was still fondly remembered as one might remember a successful party.

FREDERICK HENRY ROYCE 1863-1933

The Rolls-Royce Silver Ghost motorcar is a legend. It is the car that really began the Rolls-Royce tradition. People who have never owned a Silver Ghost, nor will ever own one, know about the fabulous car and the legend. But what is a legend, really? It is a story founded, fostered, and furthered by men. The Rolls-Royce legend is not different in that respect.

Frederick Henry Royce was born March 27, 1863. At the time of his birth, one would not have given odds that this infant would be the founder of a dynasty of fine motorcars. The Royce family was poor, and times were hard. James Royce was a miller in Alwalton, Lincolnshire, England. He could not find steady employment in the country; so the family had to pack up and move to London in 1867.

Life in the big city was not easy either, and everyone had to help in order to put food on the table. Young Henry sold newspapers instead of going to school.

In 1872 James Royce died, leaving the family with hardly tuppence to rub together. Henry had continued with his papers, and then became a telegraph boy in an effort to make more money. Like millions of working-class people around the world, the outlook for his future seemed very bleak.

At age fourteen Henry had three strokes of luck. First, he got a holiday from the telegraph office, a rare opportunity in those days. Second, he arranged to spend the holiday with his aunt at her home in Fletton. Third, his aunt was kind enough to scrape up 20 pounds to apprentice Henry to the Great Northern Railway works at nearby Peterborough. In those days, a young man had to pay the company in order to learn his trade.

Henry had a love for machinery which had started when he studied the gears, shafts, and wheels at his father's mill. Now he found an outlet for his interest, by working with the machines at the railway works. He worked hard for three years learning the rudiments of tool handling. Then his career suffered a setback.

His aunt had some hard luck and could not continue to support his apprenticeship. Sadly, Henry said goodbye to his friends in Peterborough and started to walk to the North of England to look for work. He had no home to return to in London, as his mother had become a paid housekeeper to get by.

Times were hard in England for a young man out of work. Jobs were scarce; so many applicants showed up for each opening. Henry's luck held, however, and he found a job in Leeds which paid the now incredible sum of 11 shillings for a fifty-four-hour week. One would think that a work week like that would be enough to tire anyone, but Henry Royce somehow found extra energy to pursue a new interest, electricity.

One day he spotted an advertisement in a London paper for a tester at an electric light and power company. Henry knew he had just enough money to get to London, and felt he had just enough experience to get the job. He was right on both counts.

In London again, Henry continued to budget his time and his money well. He got a room in Kentish Town and began attending Professor Ayrton's classes on electrical theory. He was so wrapped up in his job and his studies that he developed a complete lack of interest in food. He was to keep this trait all his life, much to the concern of his fellow workers in years to come.

The electric company thought so much of young Henry's ability and drive that it transferred him to its subsidiary, the Lancashire Maxim and Western Electric Company in Liverpool. He was promoted to first electrician at his new post. Then, just as things were looking good, the company went into liquidation.

Once again, Henry was faced with another sad chapter in the story of his life. He took stock of his assets. He had a solid background in electricity and mechanics; he had a lot of ambition; he had approximately 20 pounds. What he didn't have was a job; so he set about putting that right.

Henry had a good friend who was in similar straits—A. E. Claremont, who shared many interests with Henry—and the two decided to pool their money and start a business of their own. Together they had 70 pounds, which was just enough to form F. H. Royce and Company in 1884. Here again we see an interesting side of Henry's character, for the twenty-one-year-old had somehow convinced his partner to name the company after him, even though Claremont had put up more than twice his original capital.

The small electrical company opened in a tiny workshop on Cook Street in Manchester. Its products were lampholders and filaments for the fledgling electrical industry. The two partners lived in the second story of the shop. It was a happy, if meager, existence. After spending their small profits on tools and equipment there wasn't much left over for food, but Henry didn't mind that.

Things started to get better when Henry hit on a simple little electric doorbell for homeowners. The product caught on, and the orders started coming in. F. H. Royce and Company was on its way, and success was all Henry needed to put his brain to work in earnest.

First he invented a new kind of dynamo that utilized a drum-wound armature and was virtually sparkless. This remarkable new concept found a ready market in mining companies, mills, factories, and ships, where sparks could cause fires. There was only one trouble with the dynamos—they never seemed to wear out. The companies that bought them loved them, but the company that built them could have done with the extra business of replacing them. This kind of engineering refinement was another of Henry's accomplishments that was to help him in the years to come.

Electric cranes were the next big sellers, and the firm, now a limited company called Royce, Ltd., was modestly prosperous. The two original partners took advantage of their success to woo and win two sisters, whom they married in 1893. Henry and his new wife moved to Knutsford where he could take some time for a garden. He also arranged for his mother to live with him.

Business was really rolling along, but there was more and more competition, primarily due to the fact that Henry never bothered to protect his inventions. But he didn't have time for those kinds of details; he was too busy on a new love. Henry, at age forty-one, had discovered the motorcar.

It was no shock to his colleagues when, one morning in early autumn 1903, Henry announced plans to build three experimental motorcars. After numerous delays, the first Royce car was running beautifully on April 1, 1904. The car did not really represent an engineering breakthrough in the field, but it was so refined, and so well thought out, that it was quite possibly the finest motorcar in operation at that time.

Here the Royce story joins the story of Charles Stewart Rolls. In the year 1905 C. S. Rolls was selling a variety of motorcars with his partner, Claude Johnson, under the name C. S. Rolls and Company. Henry Edmunds, owner of one of the first three Royce cars, arranged for Rolls and Royce to get together so that the car could be evaluated for possible sales. The two men made an agreement, and Rolls became the agent for the new motorcar, which was to be called Rolls-Royce.

The rest of the story of Frederick Henry Royce is better known. After the success of early motorcar models, the legendary Silver Ghost was built in 1907. The car continuously improved through the years. In 1910 Charles Rolls died in an airplane crash. He had not been active in the business for some time; so his loss did not seriously affect the company. When Henry fell ill in 1911, things did not look good, because his engineering genius was still the mainstay of the firm. Henry had not taken care of his body the way he had taken care of his cars. The combination of long hours and poor food had weakened him.

Claude Johnson had become a great friend of Henry's and decided the best thing for the man and the company was a long tour of the Continent and the Near East. He had to force Henry to accompany him. The trip was a great success, and Henry's strength gradually returned. On the way home, the party stopped at Le Canadel in the south of France. Henry liked the countryside and remarked to Claude Johnson that it would be a nice place to build a house.

Mr. Johnson immediately put an architect to work, and a villa was built for Henry. He never again set foot in the Rolls-Royce factory, although his designs continued to roll in. A team of draftsmen and assistants lived and worked on the villa grounds, translating Henry's ideas into working drawings, which were sent to the Derby works to be incorporated into the product.

A second violent illness struck Henry, and he was rushed across France to a hospital in England. The problem was diagnosed as a malignant tumor. An operation saved his life, but left him a semi-invalid. Henry returned to France, and his work, after his recovery. His work and gardens were all he had left—his wife was dead, his health gone.

When World War I spread to France, Mr. Johnson arranged for Henry to return to England and live in a house near his own. Motorcar production was suspended during the war, but the Rolls-Royce contribution of armored cars, ambulances, and airplane engines greatly aided the war effort.

When the war ended Henry returned to the villa. His work went on, for he was still the genius behind every Rolls-Royce product.

In 1926, Claude Johnson, the man who had promoted Rolls-Royce cars as the best cars in the world, and the man who had saved the company by saving Henry Royce's life, died.

In 1931, Henry Royce was made a baronet. Added to his other honors, he was now Sir Frederick Henry Royce, Bart., O.B.E., M.I.M.E., in the eyes of the public. To himself, he was Henry Royce, mechanic.

Henry Royce, mechanic, died on April 22, 1933. He had lived to see his company build the standard for all automobiles. He had seen, met, and mixed with most of the royalty and high society of the world. He had led a valuable, happy, if not always healthy, life. And he had founded a legend.

CHARLES STEWART ROLLS 1877·1910

In 1904, electrical manufacturer Frederick Henry Royce produced three motorcars in a successful effort to improve on the design of his two-cylinder Decauville car. The third of these cars was bought by Mr. Henry Edmunds, a shareholder in Royce, Ltd., and a founder-member of the Automobile Club of Great Britain and Ireland. Mr. Edmunds was so impressed with his new car that he called it to the attention of one of his motoring friends who was then selling several makes of automobiles. In a few short years the friend was to foster the Rolls-Royce legend. His name, of course, was Charles Stewart Rolls.

The Honourable C. S. Rolls was born August 27, 1877. He was the third son of the first Lord and Lady Llangattock. The well-to-do family had its seat at a rambling stone mansion, the Hendre, near Monmouth, in Wales.

Being the third son, Charles was not the heir, and that may explain why so little is known of his early years. The family apparently didn't think it was necessary to record his childhood. Charles himself recalled one early incident which is enlightening so far as his later years are concerned. It seems that the family possessed an aged Bath chair which young Charles found ideal for riding wildly down the winding drive at Hendre. The object was to go as far as possible without a spill—or without hitting someone. His score for one day included a curate, a butcher's boy, and a dogcart. Spinning wheels, thrills, and excitement were things he was always seeking to the end of his days.

Charles wasn't too interested in many of the things a young aristocrat was expected to be interested in. He didn't hunt, or even shoot. Riding some of the fine horses his father produced is not mentioned in his biographies. Team sports were not his cup of tea either. He preferred to remain a loner, responsible only to himself.

In May of 1891 he entered Eton. He wasn't much of a scholar because his mind was always somewhere else. He daydreamed his time in class away, just biding time until class was out. Then he enthusiastically pursued his interests. Letters written from school portray a young man vitally interested in all kinds of new mechanical inventions. One letter persuaded his father to install an electric plant at the Hendre. Lord Llangattock built the generating station, and the Hendre became the first electrically lighted home in the county.

Leaving Eton was the time for a proper young gentleman to choose a career. Charles rejected the army and several more suggestions. He decided to take up the relatively new profession of electrical engineering. Well, yes, his tutors at Eton agreed that he did have ability in that area.

Charles wanted to study electrical engineering at Cambridge although it took a stint of tutoring to make up the essentials he had daydreamed through at Eton before he was admitted to the university. Charles took to the Cambridge life.

Initially he had an interest in cycling. As a sport it rated a Half-Blue, but all Charles really wanted was the speed and the wind in his face. He did get his Half-Blue, but never really participated fully in racing activities. His interest did a lot to boost the cycling ranks. Just the fact that a man of his station was interested in the sport was considered a boon. There just weren't enough of his "type" cycling. But once Charles discovered the motorcar, there was one less.

In 1896, Charles imported his first motorcar from France, a 3½-horsepower Peugeot. At the time, England had a 4-miles-per-hour speed limit for these newfangled machines. In addition, each car had to have three men in constant attendance. Theoretically, whenever Rolls drove his car, one man had to precede him on foot with a red flag to announce the coming of the motorcar. At night a red lantern was to be used. Naturally, in keeping with his independent nature, Charles ignored the law (or used a little highway bribery) and got away with it.

On November 14, 1896, the Locomotives on Highways Act was passed, thanks to the influence of people such as C. S. Rolls. The speed limit was raised to 12 miles per hour and the men in attendance to each motor vehicle were eliminated. Actually, Charles ignored this law also and drove his Peugeot, and later his Panhard, with such verve that he was regarded as a "scorcher."

For the next few years, the name of C. S. Rolls was connected with virtually every major motorcar event in England and Europe. He somehow found time between his motoring to complete his course of study. He was graduated from Cambridge in 1898.

By 1903, motoring had passed the pioneering phase through the efforts of Charles Rolls and his friends, who had carried on an active campaign to get as many people as possible into cars for rides. King Edward VII was an early convert. The Prince of Wales had a car soon afterwards. Charles decided it was time he went into the automobile business to reap some monetary value from the motorcar seeds he had sown.

He sold several makes of cars, both new and used, with his partner, Claude Johnson. Mr. Johnson was to become one of the most important figures in the Rolls-Royce epic. It was he who did the most to further and preserve the Rolls-Royce legend.

C. S. Rolls and Company was doing very well when Henry Edmunds approached Charles with the idea of selling the new Royce cars. Charles wasn't really too keen on the idea. He had all he could do to handle the business he had, without adding the creation of some obscure dynamo manufacturer way up in Manchester. Henry Royce, on the other hand, said he was far too busy to journey to London to see Charles. Mr. Edmunds deserves the gratitude of car enthusiasts for persisting and convincing Charles to take a day off and go to Manchester.

In May the two met in Manchester and had a good lunch before test driving the Royce car. Charles didn't like its looks, and he didn't like two-cylinder engines—until he rode in the car. His enthusiasm was so great that he drove the car to London, arriving at midnight at Claude Johnson's house. Charles woke Johnson up and insisted he go for a ride. Johnson woke up fully on the ride and agreed that the car was amazingly good.

In December, 1904, the Rolls and Royce agreement was made. Charles would take the entire output of the Manchester factory. He suggested a few changes, one being a new radiator design which is still being used. Another change was that the cars should be known as Rolls-Royce motorcars.

With his usual singleness of purpose, Charles set about making the car known. New models and improvements flowed from the shop on Cook Street. Charles put them to the test in racing and in trials. Claude Johnson began promoting sales of Rolls-Royce cars only—all the French makes were dropped. Henry Royce was building the cars, and Charles Rolls was building their reputation.

Yet, to tell the truth, Charles was getting tired of motorcars. The pioneering days had been exciting, but now the motorcar was an accepted thing. Charles began to look up for excitement.

He had been an active free-balloonist beginning in 1901. The sport was enjoyable, although certainly not as thrilling as motoring. Still, it had a certain something that attracted Charles. He became even more interested in the air when the reports reached England in 1903 that the Wright Brothers had flown a heavier-than-air machine. Charles used his ballooning as a classroom to gain data which he could use on the day when he himself would fly an airplane.

He began with gliders to learn the basic elements of powered flight. To be sure, he continued to lend his name, his presence, and his abilities to Rolls-Royce, Ltd. But the 1906 Tourist Trophy race, which he had won handily, was his last. His mind was up in the clouds.

The year 1908 found Charles flying with Wilbur Wright in France. He was the first Englishman to team up with the American fliers. More flying experience followed in his own French-built Wright biplane. In the early summer of 1910 he became the first man to complete a double crossing of the English Channel by air. On July 12, 1910, he was at Bournemouth, participating in a flying show. He crashed his fragile plane during a landing and died within seconds at the age of thirty-three.

The Rolls-Royce company and the motoring public mourned his loss. Without him, but with the prestige of his name, the company went on. What Charles had begun, Claude Johnson continued, becoming the driving force in sales, promotion, and in the maintenance of Henry Royce's health.

The Honourable C. S. Rolls had lent his reputation and considerable talent to the newborn Rolls-Royce motorcar. He lent his name as well, which gave the magical alliteration to the car he fostered. He never married. His passion as well as his love was solitary adventure. He gave the Rolls-Royce car his attention for a brief time—but his timing was perfect. Once that job was done, he moved on, as was his wont, and left the budding Rolls-Royce legend in the capable hands of Mr. Johnson and Mr. Royce. He was not forgotten, since every time you see a Rolls-Royce car, or say the name, you pay tribute to him.

THE FIRST SILVER GHOST

1907

PAINTED ESPECIALLY FOR THE JACKET . . .
THIS OFF-SIDE VIEW OF THE FIRST SILVER
GHOST AS VISUALIZED OVER THE BONNET
OF A 1910 SILVER GHOST, THE BARKER FLUSH-
SIDE TORPEDO

THE FIRST SILVER GHOST 1907

Millions of people through the automotive years have grown to love their cars. It's really quite natural to get affectionate toward a certain mechanical thing that has performed well through the years and given good service. Many times this affection comes out in the form of a name for the car.

Henry Ford's Model T became almost universally known as "Lizzie," with several sub-names such as "Jitney," "Flivver," and many more. And how many people do you know with cars named "Betsy" or "Mabel"?

According to Kenneth Ullyet, the author of *The Book of the Silver Ghost,* "The first Rolls-Royce car to have an individual name was the 20 (chassis no. 24263) sold to Captain the Honourable Guy Ward. Claude Johnson dubbed it 'Grey Ghost,' and commissioned a guild of arts and crafts to design a nameplate in repoussé style." Many other Rolls-Royce cars were given names such as "Scarlet Pimpernel," "Cookie," and even "Beauty Gal." But the best name for a Rolls-Royce was yet to come.

By 1907 the Rolls-Royce Company was committed to a "one car" policy through the foresight of Claude Johnson. The one car was the new 40/50 horsepower model. The car was a well-engineered, powerful, reliable, silent, and thoroughly elegant motorcar. All it needed was a name to match its image, and Mr. Johnson chose "Silver Ghost."

The first Silver Ghost, the car shown in this painting, was not the first 40/50 horsepower model. It was chassis number 60551, the thirteenth chassis built in the Manchester works. Mr. Johnson sent the car to Barker to be fitted with a four/five-seater touring body. The car was to be finished in aluminum, with all external fittings silverplated. A silver-plated brass plate bearing the name "Silver Ghost" was mounted on the scuttle. The finished product was a beauty—an incomparable motorcar. Mr. Rolls and Mr. Royce both knew how good the car was, and Mr. Johnson set about showing the rest of the world.

In May, 1907, the car took part in a 2,000-mile jaunt under the scrutiny of the Royal Automobile Club. The trip included the course of the forthcoming Scottish Reliability Trials, so that Mr. Johnson would have some idea of the car's performance during the trials. When the trip was over, the R.A.C. officials took the car to pieces and found only slight wear in the differential gear and the piston rings.

A month later, the car was entered in the Scottish Reliability Trials, where it won a gold medal. But Mr. Johnson didn't want to stop there. He obtained R.A.C. sanction for the car to continue on after the trials in an attempt to beat the existing nonstop record. Accordingly, the Silver Ghost was driven around the clock on a course set between London and Glasgow. According to the rules, the engine was not to be stopped except on Sundays, when the car was garaged under surveillance.

Through July and August, 1907, the grueling test continued until the agreed 15,000-mile mark was reached. The Silver Ghost had more than doubled the old record, covering 14,371 miles nonstop.

Mr. Johnson then astounded the R.A.C. officials by requesting that the car be dismantled again. He wanted to replace all the parts that showed any wear. Even he must have been astonished when it cost two pounds, two shillings, and seven pence to put the Silver Ghost in a like-new condition. Mr. Johnson had certainly made his point about the quality of the Rolls-Royce Silver Ghost.

In 1907, *The Autocar* said of the Silver Ghost, "At whatever speed this car is being driven on its direct third, there is *no* engine as far as sensation goes, nor are one's auditory nerves troubled driving or standing by a fuller sound than emanates from an eight-day clock." And later, ". . . . there is no realisation of driving propulsion; the feeling as the passenger sits either at the front or the back of the vehicle is one of being wafted through the landscape."

The painter has properly placed the Silver Ghost in front of its home, the first factory on Cook Street, Manchester, where all the pioneer work on the 40/50 horse-power model was done. The torn poster on the brick wall reminds us that F. H. Royce and Company manufactured electric cranes, dynamos, and other electric equipment before Mr. Royce became intrigued by the motorcar. Mr. Rolls and Mr. Royce are pictured in the glass case. Of the two smaller paintings the top one depicts the first Rolls-Royce car sold to a private owner—a 10-horsepower, two-cylinder model of 1904. The other is one of the first three Royce two-cylinder cars.

After the excitement of the nonstop run by the Silver Ghost had died down a bit, the orders began coming in for other cars. The name Silver Ghost stuck, and is now applied to all of the 40/50 horsepower models, including the twelve built before the Silver Ghost.

Shortly after its great success, Mr. Dan Hanbury bought the Silver Ghost from the factory. In the course of many years he covered an additional 400,000 miles in it before Rolls-Royce reacquired the car in 1948. To date the car has completed over half a million miles and is still in perfect running order. The Honourable C. S. Rolls' silver-plated oil lamps are mounted on the scuttle. The car may be seen at Number 14 Conduit Street, London.

ROLLS ROYCE Lᵀᴰ

ROLLS ROYCE Lᵀᴰ

Melbourne Brindle

THE MAUDSLAY-BODIED SHOOTING BRAKE 1907

Several times in this book we speak about the fact that Rolls-Royce built only the chassis and that owners had to have bodies built to their taste. What hasn't been written is that this separate chassis-body relationship had certain advantages for the purchaser.

If a Rolls-Royce Silver Ghost owner had been pleased with the performance and operation of his motorcar, he might want to keep it for a long time. Rolls-Royce mechanical parts were very long-lived, and a car with many thousand miles could be considered just nicely broken-in. Yet, styles changed as often in those days as they do now, and the owner might have preferred the body lines of a more recent car over those of his own. It was a simple matter to have a new body fitted to the old chassis. Voilà! Instant contemporary motorcar.

On the other hand, this complicated body interchange could take place from car to car in the same period. There were many other makes of motorcar being produced during the period covered by this book. A Silver Ghost owner conceivably could have wanted to replace the body on his car with a body from another make. That is exactly what happened with the car in this painting.

Silver Ghost chassis number 577 was delivered from the Rolls-Royce works at Manchester to Hooper Coachbuilders in London in 1907. The purchaser, Mr. Baird, related to Viscount Stonehaven of Durris Lodge, Deeside, Aberdeenshire, ordered a chauffeur-driven landaulet body. The car was to be painted dark blue. It was delivered some time later, and Mr. Baird must have been pleased with his new "motor" made by that new company, Rolls-Royce.

Mr. Baird must have enjoyed the car, because by 1911 he had a companion Silver Ghost, a 1911 touring car. He also had a Panhard et Levassor landaulet and a 1906 Maudslay shooting brake in his motorhouse. Mr. Baird preferred the 1907 Ghost chassis over all the others, but he also liked the Maudslay's shooting brake body. So, he combined the two and ended up with a car that pleased him all around.

Mr. Baird's chauffeur, David Hart, treated all the cars in the motorhouse as though they were his own. His favorite also was the Ghost shooting brake. He named her "the Auld Lady," a name which has stayed with her through the years.

The Auld Lady was saved from destruction twice during her long career. A shooting brake is the British equivalent of a station wagon, a real country car to be used for hunting or for utility work. During World War I, someone thought it would be a good idea to saw off the rear portion of the Maudslay body to make it easier to carry firewood from the hills. A last-minute stay of execution halted the hand on the saw. The double molding to the rear of the front seat hides the small damage that was done.

During World War II, RAF personnel billeted on the estate started a fire in a corner of the motorhouse to keep warm. The fire soon got out of hand, and before it could be extinguished, the paint on the near side of the car was blistered and the front tire was burned to ashes.

Mr. James P. Smith took delivery of the Auld Lady from the late Mr. Baird's granddaughter in 1955. Coincidentally, the first rally he participated in with the car was in Manchester, the place where she was built. Many more rallies and events followed, but the most significant was the first Kildrummy Castle Rally on Donside in 1958.

During the rally, Mr. Smith learned that David Hart, the Auld Lady's chauffeur, was still alive and residing in Deeside. Mr. Hart had wanted to come and see "his" car, but he was eighty-three, and his doctor had forbidden the journey. Mr. Smith surprised the old gentleman by driving to Mr. Hart's home. A joyful reunion took place, with Mr. Smith gaining some valuable information about the early years of the Auld Lady as Mr. Hart reminisced.

As Mr. Smith prepared to leave, Mr. Hart exclaimed happily, "Well, I could not come to Kildrummy to see the Auld Lady, but instead the Auld Lady has been to see me!"

As she now stands, the Auld Lady is one of the most original of the early Silver Ghosts. Since most of her life was spent in Scotland, she was never returned to the Manchester or Derby works for the modifications and improvements which came fast and furious during the early Silver Ghost years. (Indeed, Claude Johnson at one time suggested to the Rolls-Royce board that every Silver Ghost chassis be guaranteed unconditionally against obsolescence. Luckily the suggestion was turned down.)

The car still retains her original wheels and springs. Even the Rolls-Royce company's original Silver Ghost has had modifications in those areas. If you compare the springs on the two cars, you will see that those on the Auld Lady are curved, while those on the company car are quite flat. The Auld Lady, like other 1907 Ghosts, uses two different tire sizes. The front tires are 880 × 120, and the rear are 895 × 135.

This is one of the two cars in the book that does not have the traditional polished aluminum panel behind the bonnet—the other being Queen Mary's Silver Ghost.

The Auld Lady may still be found in Scotland, at least part of each year, when Mr. Smith is in residence at his home near ancient Kildrummy Castle, pictured as a background in this painting. Above the weathered window hangs a shotgun by Purdey —considered by many to be the Rolls-Royce of firearms makers. The SU 45 number plate is from the Auld Lady's motorhouse companion, the 1911 touring car, which no longer exists.

Tacked on the wall is the certificate of merit given to chauffeur David Hart in 1924 by Rolls-Royce, Ltd. It certifies that he, as driver-mechanic, had "paid attention" to cars numbered 577 and 1633 during the 88,274 miles they were driven from 1907 to 1924. It is signed by Claude Johnson. Rolls-Royce also presented Mr. Hart with the enameled brooch bearing the red *RR* initials. When Mr. Hart died, his widow presented both of these items to Mr. Smith. She probably felt that these mementos of his should be kept somewhere near "his" car, the Auld Lady.

SU·45

CERTIFICATE of MERIT
ISSUED BY ROLLS·ROYCE LTD
TO DRIVER·MECHANICS OF
PRIVATELY OWNED ROLLS·ROYCE CARS

Period November 1907.
to April 1924

This is to certify that from
information received from
the owner, and from inspections made by our officials,
we are of opinion that the
attention paid by Driver
Mechanic David Hart
to the privately owned
six·cylinder Rolls·Royce cars
No. 577 & 1633 has been,
excellent over a total of 88,274 miles.

For ROLLS·ROYCE LTD
C. Johnson
GENERAL MANAGING DIRECTOR

MOTOR UNION

ROYAL AUTOMOBILE CLUB ASSOCIATE
ROYAL SCOTTISH AUTOMOBILE CLUB

ROLLS·ROYCE LTD
LONDON & MANCHESTER
No. 577

RR

SU·76

Maudslay Motor Co Ltd
PARKSIDE   COVENTRY

THE PEARL OF THE EAST 1908

In 1600 the English Sovereign granted a charter to a group of English merchants who wished to open commerce with India. Privileges were also granted by ruling Indian princes, and the East India Company gained a foothold there which eventually led to total domination of that country after years of diplomacy and war.

Employees of the company and military personnel who had been stationed there returned to England with vivid tales of life in "Inja." By the late nineteenth century, writers such as Rudyard Kipling were bringing the world, and words, of India into every English home. One word above all caught the imagination—*maharajah*.

Maharajah, a prince of India. The word conjured up visions of immense wealth, graceful palaces, hordes of servants, harems of veiled beauties, and tiger hunts from the backs of elephants. One particular Englishman had visions of his own—visions of a ready market for a new commodity, the motorcar.

Mr. Frank J. Norbury of Manchester decided to introduce the new Silver Ghost of Rolls-Royce to India in 1907. Mr. Norbury was retired from his own printing business, whose major product had been brightly colored labels which were attached to fabrics destined for China and India.

Obviously a man of action, Mr. Norbury promptly ordered a chassis from the Cook Street, Manchester, factory of Rolls-Royce. The chassis was just as promptly built. It was the thirty-seventh 40/50 horsepower model made, number 60576.

The chassis was delivered, which meant driven in those days, to Joseph Cockshoot & Co., Ltd., in Manchester to be fitted with an unusual portable-top limousine body according to Mr. Norbury's specifications. Although this writer has seen no pictures of the car in open form, it is assumed that the entire roof of the car was removable from the point just above the vertical stripes. When completed, the unique limousine was named "Pearl of the East."

Fortunately for us, Mr. C. W. Morton, long acknowledged as the Rolls-Royce company biographer, obtained valuable information from Mr. Andrew Bottomley, who built most of the body at Cockshoot's. The car had a folding luggage carrier at the rear, combined with a seat for a servant. (Pity the servant who had to sit amidst the dust when riding on the roads of that period.) A roof rack carried a matched set of Finnigan trunks in brown leather. One spare tire had its own Finnigan case which rode above the driver. The other spare endured the elements.

The passenger section featured ventilators above each side window—the ancestor of our flow-through ventilation systems. The entire interior was trimmed in supple brown leather.

When finished, the Pearl of the East was shipped to India by Mr. Norbury. It was the first Rolls-Royce to appear in that country, and it made quite an impression, just as Mr. Norbury knew it would.

The car was exhibited to the public at the 1908 Bombay Motor Show. It motored away with the first prize for appearance. Not satisfied to stop there, Mr. Norbury heard that the Motor Union of Western India was putting on a reliability trial. He entered the Pearl of the East in class five of the competition.

This was to be Mr. Norbury's supreme test for the Silver Ghost. He had already established that the car was a "looker"; now to see if it was a "goer" too.

The trial route covered a lot of tough terrain. The course wound 620 miles, starting at Bombay, through six passes in the western Ghats mountains, to Kolhapur. No tools or spares were carried, and the bonnet was locked. An official observer riding in the car had the key.

Although this painting shows the car in closed form, the top was removed for the race. The Pearl of the East completed the trial without a single involuntary stop and won the event easily. Surely this has to be the most luxurious automobile ever to win a race. *The Autocar* certainly felt that way at the time when it reported, "The Rolls-Royce created a unique record in the annals of motoring." The car won the Mysore cup, two gold medals, a silver cup, and two diplomas for its performance.

After this display of reliability matched with beauty, Mr. Norbury did not have long to wait for a buyer. The Maharajah of Gwalior bought the car and began another kind of race—the race by the princes of India to see which one could outdo the others in purchasing, adorning, and amassing Rolls-Royce motorcars.

The Nizam of Hyderabad was one of those smitten by the Pearl of the East. At that time he was supposed to be the wealthiest man in the world. His initial stock of fantastically ornamented Rolls-Royce cars was passed on to his heir, the Prince of Berar, along with a love for the marque. By the 1950s, the Nizam's collection was reputed to number fifty Rolls-Royces.

In 1911 the Indian Government ordered eight Silver Ghosts to use as state carriages for King George V and Queen Mary during the coronation ceremonies at the Delhi Durbar. Rolls-Royce lent a team of drivers for the cars.

Through the years, the princes of India have been staunch in their devotion to Rolls-Royce. His Highness the Maharajah Kumer of Vizianagram ordered one fitted with special equipment for night hunting, including swiveling headlights on each running board for tiger shooting. His Royal Highness the Maharajah of Patiala once had a motorshed with twenty-two Rolls-Royce models awaiting his selection.

In 1921 or 1922, the Nawab of Rampur ordered three identical Silver Ghosts with touring bodies by the Grosvenor Carriage Company. Each was fitted with an outrigged seat just ahead of the front door on the near side.

The Maharajah of Mysore owned several fabulous Rolls-Royce cars, one of which can be seen in this book. It was he who donated the Mysore cup won by the Pearl of the East.

The upper painting in the lower left shows the Honourable C. S. Rolls winning the 1906 Tourist Trial, thus gaining the first competitive victory for the fledgling firm. The lower scene shows the Gardens of Shalimar in Lahore built by Shah Jahan for Mumtaz Mahal, his beloved wife.

Through the vision of Mr. Norbury, Rolls-Royce cars gained great success in India. Unaccountably, he did not pursue his first success, and even his beautiful Pearl of the East has disappeared.

EAST
1908

Melbourne Brindle

SILVER GHOST USED BY H.R.H. QUEEN MARY 1908

Ask the average person which maker of automobiles has supplied the official cars to British royalty for the last sixty years. Chances are excellent that the answer will be "Rolls-Royce, right?"

Wrong. Until Her Majesty Queen Elizabeth II chose a Rolls-Royce Phantom IV as her official means of transportation in 1952, all Britain's reigning monarchs had used Daimler automobiles. This apparent exclusivity was no doubt mere force of habit, for the first British royal personage to own a motorcar was King Edward VII, and his first car was a Daimler.

King Edward had been one of the early motorists in England. In 1899, as Prince of Wales, he had gone for his initial motoring trip with Mr. Douglas-Scott-Montagu, later the second Lord Montagu of Beaulieu. A photograph was taken at the time showing Prince Edward sitting high up on the 12-horsepower Daimler, jaunty cap on head and cigar in hand.

Queen Victoria did not approve of the Prince's interests in these newfangled devices. She had seen another photograph of him in a motorcar when the tall hat he was wearing had been blown or shaken over his nose. She told her Master of Horse, "I hope you will never allow any of those horrible machines to be used in my stables. I am told that they smell exceedingly nasty, and are very shaky and disagreeable conveyances altogether."

None of this dimmed the Prince's enthusiasm for motoring, and a later report tells of Queen Victoria ordering her horses to be paraded around the stable yard while a motorcar was running to accustom them to the noise and smell.

Upon the death of Queen Victoria in 1901, motoring in England got a kingly booster. King Edward got his first Daimler that year. The motorcar was specially built for him and he used to drive it to Windsor to spend his weekends. Like most motorists in those unreliable automotive days, the King knew something of the mechanical operation of his motorcar. Once, while attempting a longer trip to Sandringham, the Daimler developed tire trouble at Finley and had to be hauled unroyally by horses to a bicycle shop to be repaired.

In 1905 the King became the patron of the automobile exhibition at the Crystal Palace, where the very newest examples of motorcar genius were displayed. With his approval, in 1907, the Automobile Club of Great Britain and Ireland became the Royal Automobile Club.

King Edward had many motorcars. Although he stuck to Daimler for official duties, it was well known that he favored his Mercedes for personal use. His wife, Queen Alexandra, had a 1906 Renault which she kept in use for twenty years, long after the death of her husband.

In 1900 the Honourable Charles S. Rolls had an opportunity to impress another future king and queen with a motorcar. The Duke and Duchess of York, later King George V and Queen Mary, visited Rolls' home, the Hendre, in October of that year. Regardless of his father's feelings, the Duke was not yet a motoring convert. The Duchess had even written a letter at one time in which she mentioned meeting up with "an odious motor-car which smelt so nasty and made such a noise."

During the short trip in Rolls' Panhard the royal couple apparently found that they liked motoring. *The Autocar* reported, "Her Royal Highness showed no sense of nervousness, and seemed happiest when the speed was highest down some clear slope."

When King Edward took the throne, the Duke and Duchess became Prince and Princess of Wales. By 1903 the couple had purchased their own motorcar—a Daimler.

When King George V ascended the throne in 1910, he and his Queen were completely sold on the motorcar. Queen Mary, especially, had taken an interest in mechanical things and had a curiosity, unique among queens and queen consorts, to find out how things worked. She was the first queen consort ever to delve into the working man's world and took every opportunity to visit factories, collieries, and industrial exhibits.

While the Daimler remained the official royal motorcar, the reputation of Rolls-Royce was recognized, even in the Royal Palace. In 1911 semiofficial royal approval was given to purchase eight Rolls-Royce landaulets for the Delhi Durbar in India, where the King and Queen would be crowned again at coronation ceremonies for the empire.

When World War I began, the royal family came closer to the hearts of British citizens by sending two sons, both destined to be kings of England, into the struggle. Edward (King Edward VIII) and Albert (King George VI) went to war, and so did the King and Queen. King George made frequent trips to the front, where he always traveled by Rolls-Royce. Queen Mary did her part by visiting hospitals within Britain to comfort wounded fighting men.

In 1917 Queen Mary accompanied the King to France. She had heard of many important visitors who had gone on "joy rides" to the battlefields, staying far from the ugliness of the war. She would have none of that, and insisted on visiting hospitals where the most seriously wounded cases were undergoing treatment. Working on behalf of the International Red Cross, she visited hospitals day after day in France and Belgium. This Rolls-Royce was her royal transportation.

The car was a formal landaulet, adaptable to either open or closed touring. A friend of the painter who was an American volunteer nurse in the British Army vividly recalls seeing Queen Mary arrive at Red Cross headquarters in this Silver Ghost. The car is unique in two ways: It features a varnished hardwood panel at the rear of the bonnet (polished aluminum was the norm) and Rudge-Whitworth wire wheels. Few Rolls-Royce cars have these, Dunlop being the usual supplier.

Queen Mary's royal insignia hangs in front of the windscreen. An acetylene searchlight, acetylene generating tank, spare tire, and Red Cross flag help make this already imposing limousine seem even taller.

This Silver Ghost has disappeared without a trace, but Queen Mary lived to see her granddaughter formally acknowledge what the rest of the world had thought for years—that Rolls-Royce was the car of English royalty.

THE "BALLOON CAR" OF C. S. ROLLS 1909

Air travel is now the fastest way to get from point A to point B, for the average person. After leaving the ground with an ear-splitting roar, the passenger cannot escape the sounds of the wind whistling past, the stereo music, the conversation, the air conditioning, and maybe the movie. Supersonic aircraft wait in the wings to carry passengers faster and more noisily through the sky, while even the earth will be bombarded with noise from sonic booms.

There was a time when traveling through the air was sport. Those who could afford to play soared high above the earth in absolute silence, their direction controlled by capricious breezes. Man had not yet perfected wings, engines, and controls; so balloons were used to play the game.

The balloon has been called a typically Edwardian phenomenon because it was so entirely unhurried and basically carefree. When that definition is applied to the life of C. S. Rolls, it becomes a contradiction. Rolls sought adventure, and, from contemporary reports of ballooning, it would be hard to find too much adventure in the sport. Since the Wright brothers' flight in 1903, Rolls had been interested in flying; so perhaps his balloon passion was educational. As a primer for powered flight, ballooning would have supplied him with knowledge of winds and weather. Still Rolls was not one to champion lost causes, and it was obvious that ballooning was going nowhere fast (or perhaps that should be slow). So most historians deduce that he just must have enjoyed riding in balloons.

Balloons of the great years—1905 to 1908—were made by filling a fragile silk "envelope" with up to 50,000 cubic feet of coal gas. Ascents were naturally limited to locations near a gas works. Up to four passengers (depending on their weight) rode in a woven rattan basket, known as a "car," suspended beneath the envelope. Various ropes and sand ballast bags were also carried on the car to control ascent and descent somewhat.

Ascents were made by jettisoning ballast until the proper rate of climb was achieved. Direction was then purely a matter of chance, and the well-equipped aeronaut carried *Bradshaw's Railway Guide* to help locate his position and also to indicate the nearest rail service he could use to return home.

After "valving" gas to descend, the aeronaut would carefully fold the deflated envelope, stow it in the car, and find some means of transport for himself, his passengers, and his balloon to the nearest railroad station.

C. S. Rolls solved the return problem by having his Silver Ghost set up as a balloon tender. The motorcar served two purposes. It kept track of the balloon's progress from the ground so that the driver could come up quickly and lend Rolls a hand with the packing-up procedure. Then, with the smaller balloons, the Ghost would be used to carry the aeronaut and his craft home.

Rolls' one-man balloon, "Imp," of 17,500-cubic-foot capacity, was carried on the

Ghost this way. A glance at the painted "snapshot" in the painting shows "Imp" packed and ready for the return trip. The gentleman on the near side is Mr. Short, pioneer balloonist, and maker of Rolls' balloons.

The chassis of this Ghost was almost as unusual as the purpose for which Rolls had Mulliner build the body. It was one of four special models built in the summer of 1908 to provide 70 horsepower—as against 48 horsepower for production models. The engine featured overhead inlet valves and a longer stroke to give a higher compression ratio.

Two of these motorcars were entered in the 2,000-mile International Touring Car Trial that summer. The cars, named "White Knave" and "Silver Rogue," had to complete a specific course and then travel to the Brooklands track where a 200-mile speed competition against the clock would finish the trial. White Knave broke a piston, but Silver Rogue, driven by Percy Northey, won its class easily. Incidentally, the names were given to the cars because the competition allowed the cars to run without silencers, and Rolls-Royce, Ltd., did not want to sully the reputation of the silent Silver Ghost.

Although the 70-horsepower models never became standard, the balloon car of C. S. Rolls has had its imitators. The original model has disappeared without a trace, but many veteran car fanciers have built replicas to carry on the design.

A photograph of the balloon car exists with Rolls at the wheel and H. J. Mulliner in the passenger seat. At the time this painting was being started, Mr. Mulliner was alive, and, at ninety-three years of age, this last surviving founder of the Automobile Club of Great Britain and Ireland supplied important information about the body of the car. His letter is reproduced at the rear of this book. Mr Mulliner has since died.

The mudguards on the balloon car are unique in that they are metal in front and glossy black patent leather in the rear. Also, the Rudge-Whitworth wire wheels should be noted since they were seldom found on a Rolls-Royce.

One can easily ask the reason why a person would devote so much time and money to an apparently dull sport like ballooning—even to the extent of building a motorcar to complement the hobby. Lord Montagu of Beaulieu may have supplied the simplest answer in his book, *Rolls of Rolls-Royce*. He tells of one occasion when a balloon crew was lost and descended low enough to hail a passing teenager and ask, "Where are we?" The teenager replied innocently, "Why, you are up in a balloon!" And indeed, for Rolls and his fellow balloon enthusiasts, that must have been reason enough.

Charles Stewart Rolls
1877-1910

BARKER FLUSH-SIDE TORPEDO PHAETON 1910

If ever anything possesses built-in obsolescence, it's a luxury automobile. The fact that a limousine *is* a limousine marks it for a quick comedown, because the people who could afford to buy it in the first place can afford to get rid of it and get a new one without blinking an eye. And somehow the market for used limousines quickly dries up after a car is just a few years old.

Old limousines are ideal for conversion to ambulances, campers, and transports for rock music groups. They're great conversation pieces for suburban eccentrics—but they hardly fit in the garage. And did you ever notice how many ten-year-old limousines you can see decaying in poverty areas where they fill the need for cheap transportation that will carry a family of fifteen?

Sadly, this pattern of loss is nothing new. While we may not mourn the slow destruction of a 1959 Cadillac limousine, we would probably rise up en masse to prevent a car such as this Rolls-Royce Silver Ghost from being sold to power pumps in a coal mine. Yet that's just what happened to this car.

When chassis number 1298 rolled out of the Rolls-Royce Derby works on May 3, 1910, it was assured a bright future. After all, a Rolls-Royce was *the* car to own if you were rich and liked to travel in a luxurious manner. And this Rolls-Royce went to the Barker coachbuilding firm to be fitted with a magnificent touring body. The price was approximately £1200—a tidy sum in 1910.

In 1919, after the war was all over, the car was then nine years old—out-of-date, old-fashioned. It was sold to the Dunlop Rubber Company to be used, not for regal transportation, but for tire-testing.

In 1920 the car was sold to a gentleman in North Wales. There are no facts to back up the statement, but it is doubtful that this gentleman could have afforded the car when new.

For fifteen years the Silver Ghost whispered along the hills and valleys of Wales. Then it was sold to a Welsh colliery company. Apparently no one protested. The company had a problem with water seeping into its mine shafts and needed a reliable engine to power the pumps. What could be more reliable than a Rolls-Royce engine?

Happily, the company never put its plan into action. The previous owner repurchased the car in 1936, but never used it again.

Mr. S. J. Skinner of Basingstoke, Hampshire, discovered the car in 1947. What he saw was a thirty-seven-year-old luxury car. No longer out-of-date—on the contrary, it was sought after. Mr. Skinner no doubt recognized the straight front axle and could date the car from 1910 when that feature began. It was a three-speed Ghost. It was quite a find.

Under Mr. Skinner's care, No. 1298 was restored to pristine glory. For many years this Ghost has been an active and outstanding participant in veteran car events both in and out of Great Britain.

The car made a 2,500-mile tour of the Continent in 1950, including climbs to several Alpine passes. From Geneva a 475-mile run was made to Dunkirk in fifteen hours—this in the car's fortieth year.

In 1954 the car was one of twelve Edwardian and vintage cars in the Vintage Sports Car Club's competition with American cars of similar age which were touring England. The Barker-bodied beauty was also a member of the return British team which visited the United States in 1957. It won the Concours d'Élégance in New York, and then participated in a 1,000-mile tour and competition in New England. Mr. Skinner still actively "campaigns" his Ghost. It resides in his motorshed with two other Silver Ghosts, plus a Rolls-Royce Twenty and a Phantom II.

The gear ratios are 2.9, 5, and 7.9:1. The car's maximum speed is 60 to 65 miles per hour. Ignition is by low-tension coil and high-tension magneto. It still gets 11 miles per gallon of petrol. The hood is of the "one-man Kodalapso" type, which probably took four men twenty minutes to erect.

If you appreciate this book of paintings, this is the car to thank. The painter saw it when it visited the United States in 1957. Only a painting would satisfy his feelings for the car. From that beginning the book developed.

The painter included the paddle steamer *Ozone* in the painting because he remembered it in all its Edwardian glory in Port Phillip Bay. The Taj Mahal represents beauty in manmade form, as does the car. The items at lower left are relics of the British Empire during the period when this Ghost was new.

Here, then, is a luxury car which has gone full circle: from valued possession, to workhorse, to abuse, to disuse, to discovery, to valued possession. Sadly, it is one of the few. We are fortunate to have it with us still.

R-1910

Melbourne Brindle

SELF-DRIVING PHAETON WITH DICKEY SEAT 1911

For the majority of Americans, the fun of driving an automobile can be traced back to the end of World War II. Servicemen who had been stationed in England and Europe returned home with tales of the small, spidery cars whose performance belied their size. Many others brought more than the stories, they brought the cars: MGs, H.R.G.s, Singers, Frazer-Nashes, Rileys, and others. In the late forties and early fifties, driving one of those little "furrin" cars was enough to cause an accident involving one or more gawking motorists.

They were called "sports cars." And that was the whole idea. These cars proved to Americans that driving could be sport. You could get in one and lose yourself in a world where you were in control and communed with the road. It was a very satisfying experience.

It is not surprising that the cars which began the automotive revolution in the United States came mostly from England. The English have long been known for their independent nature as well as their love of sport. Proper control of a motorcar became as natural as breathing for those who could afford to own one. But even in England it hadn't always been this way.

Motoring began in England as a rich man's fad. The cars were frightfully expensive, and as they were unreliable as well, it required even more money to keep one running. When men such as Charles Rolls and Douglas-Scott-Montagu were pitting their motorcars against each other at the turn of the century, those gentlemen were doing the driving. After all, what was the fun of owning such a toy unless one could play with it?

Still, when it came to traveling in style, most of the wealthy and titled Englishmen relied on their horse-drawn carriages. Motorcars were noisy, made great clouds of evil-smelling smoke, and often broke down in the most discommoding fashion. One couldn't consider taking a lady in one of those contraptions!

The pioneer motorists were anxious to gain wider acceptance of their vehicles. Many, like Charles Rolls, had gone into the business of selling motorcars; so it became important to refine the mechanism. Men of mechanical genius, Henry Royce and others, came forward and produced new designs that filled the bill.

The transportation trend was starting to swing toward the motorcar by 1907. Beautiful matched-horse teams were put out to pasture, and the carriage was replaced with an elegant motorcar of the Rolls-Royce Silver Ghost type. Drivers and footmen became chauffeurs. Instead of rubbing down horses and cleaning and polishing harness, chauffeurs were sent to schools operated by the manufacturers to learn the care and handling of motorcars.

By 1914 there were a great number of people who were conveyed by motorcar, but did not know how to operate one. As Anthony Bird and Ian Hallows mention in their book, *The Rolls-Royce Motor Car*, "The Silver Ghost, particularly in closed form, had been thought of almost exclusively as the province of the paid driver, as it was,

52

of course, contrary to the etiquette of the time for any but a liveried servant to be seen in command of a formal limousine or landaulet. Although open-bodied versions might occasionally be conducted by their owners the chauffeur was usually still in evidence."

Anyone doing research on motorcars during this period will be surprised to see such obvious mention made of well-known personages who did know how to drive. Baron Rothschild gave his Ghost to the British war effort in 1914 and took driving lessons so he could drive the officers assigned to it around the front lines. During the war, the Prince of Wales's driver was killed by shrapnel, so the Prince, who knew how to drive, drove the dead man's body to a casualty station and continued his tour of the front.

So, it is with some understanding that we come to this painting and the unusual phrase, "self-driving phaeton." This beautiful car was obviously designed and built by Rolls-Royce and Hooper & Company, Ltd., to be driven by its owner, Roland Foster, Esq.

Basically this Ghost carried only two people in the front compartment. For occasional extra passengers, the flat rear deck held a surprise—a folding "dickey seat" which could be raised in position for two more riders. Hopefully they did not have to ride far, exposed to the wind and weather as they would have been. The ride must have been exciting, for, as you can see, the bottom cushion of the seat is held in place by two strong leather straps.

This is the only car in this book fitted with Jacquet-Maurel & Condac double shock absorbers on the rear springs. These accessories could only be fitted to Silver Ghosts with three-quarter elliptic springs.

Resting on the windowsill are items which the painter felt might have been typical possessions of the kind of man who drove his own Rolls-Royce in 1911. The small wooden box contains a Bosch DR-6 magneto kit—a complete maintenance kit used to care for the Bosch magnetos used on Rolls-Royce Silver Ghosts.

BOSCH TYPE DR6

TULIP-BACKED LIMOUSINE 1911

There is always a certain excitement that occurs to some of us when a modern limousine passes. Up front sits the chauffeur, confident and always haughty in his livery. Hidden mysteriously, deep in the back seat, is "the person" who must be someone important to have such a car and driver at his beck and call. One can imagine all sorts of things about this obviously wealthy individual—from movie star, to government dignitary, to Mafia leader. It's a wonderful game to play, this game of "Who-is-it-in-the-limousine?"

And when one takes a walk down Fifth Avenue in New York City and passes by Tiffany's or Cartier's, the long black cars wait along the curb. The chauffeurs, who have a caste system all their own, talk only to one another, never to you. If you are romantic-ally inclined you almost want to linger (read loiter) there to watch the ladies sweep out of the shops, furs flying, to enter the limousine doors which are always open for them as they reach the cars.

In the last few years more and more people have gained the means to enjoy the luxury of a limousine and a chauffeur. As the number of people in the upper middle class has grown, so has the economy that enables people to afford things that were once the province of the wealthy upper class.

When the Rolls-Royce Silver Ghost was in its golden era, the distinction between classes was very great. There were a few "haves" and millions of "have-nots." With that in mind it is easy to imagine the impression that a formal limousine of the type in this painting must have had on the English workingman in 1911. Most were no doubt awed by the ponderous vehicle wafting past on the road. Others may have been saddened, knowing that their station in life would always be the same and that they would never have even a small fraction of the price of a motorcar such as that. Still others, scant few others, may have set their minds on one day owning a possession such as a Silver Ghost. One wonders how many achieved their dream.

Mrs. S. Benger (of the Benger's food firm) ordered a chassis in 1911 from her friend Henry Royce. She lived at the Grange, Knutsford, Cheshire, and was a close neighbor of Royce's while the Manchester factory was still in operation.

Chassis number 1534 was built at the Derby works and sent to Joseph Lawton, coachbuilder, to be finished. The result was the stunning formal limousine finished with the distinctive tulip-backed rear body style which you see here.

It is easy to imagine that even Mrs Benger was thrilled when this limousine first whispered to a halt at her doorstep. This was an era when cost was no object, and brass and copper were in evidence on motorcars. The car was and is the essence of Edwardian elegance.

The color is crimson lake, which was put on by brush in those days with a finish difficult to match with even the most expensive of today's spray paint jobs. Master painters knew how to load their brushes heavily with paint and flow it on, using just enough to give the finish depth, yet not too much to run and sag. Never a brush mark, ever!

Then came the lining, the painted accents that enhanced the moldings and other details of the car. Fine lining brushes with a unique asymmetric tapering shape were dipped in paint of just the right consistency and wiped repeatedly on a test surface until the line was perfect. Only then would the steady-handed craftsman lay the stripe on the body. Fine vermilion outlined the wider black linings to add even more elegance to this motorcar masterpiece.

When Mrs. Benger entered the car she found all the comforts of home. Cut crystal bud vases, always filled with flowers in season, added their color and perfume to the fawn broadcloth upholstery and burl walnut paneling.

Privacy? A pull on the tassels above each rear window brought down shades to enclose the interior. A change of plans? A whisper into a small silver trumpet which carried her commands to a duplicate trumpet right near the chauffeur's ear. Excursion, perhaps? The matched luggage rode atop the car with the spare tire. When night fell, the limousine could be lighted like a palace on wheels, with oil pillar and side lights and acetylene headlights.

In 1920, the executor of Mrs. Benger's estate sold the car to a renowned Manchester doctor, J. Howson Ray. Little is known of it during the time it was owned by Dr. Ray. Suddenly in 1945 it came to light again.

Dr. Ray's daughter wrote to Rolls-Royce explaining that her father's old Silver Ghost was lying unused in the back portion of the coach house. Did the car, she wanted to know, have any historic or monetary value? Naturally it did, so Rolls-Royce passed her letter on to Mr. Stanley Sears, noted Rolls-Royce collector. Mr. Sears journeyed to Manchester to see the car and bought it on the spot. He brought it back to his museum in Bolney.

In 1949, Mr. W. F. Watson bought the car from Mr. Sears, transported it to his seaside home in Aldwick, Bognor Regis, West Sussex. There the car was restored to showroom condition. The chauffeur's seat still uses the original leather covering. The tassels and shades in the rear compartment are also original. The broadcloth upholstery is an authentic replacement, and lace antimacassars protect it just as they did when the car was new.

The tasteful opulence of the enclosed motorcars built before World War I marks the high point in limousine construction. These vehicles combined the best of the horsedrawn carriage-builder's art with the silent mechanical performance of the newer motorcar-manufacturer's skill. One view of a car such as this and the viewer has no doubt what it was, and what it was meant to do.

ESTO·QUOD·ESSE·VIDERIS

LONDON–EDINBURGH MODEL 1911

There's really nothing new under the sun. Every well-informed car enthusiast knows the story of the millions of dollars poured into auto racing by the Ford Motor Company in the last few years in its successful effort to gain a performance image. He knows how Ford tried to buy out the great Ferrari, and, failing that, went on to build the great Ford GT-40 cars that dominated long-distance road racing for a few years.

The goal was performance. The money was spent and the goal was achieved. People who bought new Fords were encouraged to believe that some of that glory rubbed off on their new Falcon, or Thunderbird. And those folks with money to burn could even buy a replica of the GT-40 to tool around town.

Rolls-Royce had a similar experience with Napier early in its history. From the start of the motorcar industry, Napier had been a dominant marque. Before there was a Rolls-Royce car or company, Charles Rolls was racing his Panhard against faster cars built by Montague Napier. By the time Rolls-Royce started producing the Silver Ghost, Napier was the leading motorcar in England.

The men at Rolls-Royce, Ltd., were a persistent lot. By 1910 they had pitted their car against every comer and had come out the winner. Trial after trial, race after race, hill climb after hill climb the Rolls-Royce reputation was being made. And Napier was coming out at the short end of the comparison. Rolls-Royce had a smoother-running engine than the Napier's. The Silver Ghost was a better-looking car too, since the Napier's long engine required the radiator to be way ahead of the front axle and this made the body look all out of proportion.

Napier still had an edge—in fact it had three edges. One was speed, one was top gear performance, and the third was Selwyn Edge, a racing driver of great renown. Edge had enjoyed great success in Napier cars and was determined to keep it. He encouraged Montague Napier to enter a car in a top-gear-only run from London to Edinburgh. The Royal Automobile Club observed the run. The car was a slightly hopped-up 65-horsepower Napier with a 2.7:1 final gear ratio. As part of the test, fuel consumption was to be recorded, and after the Edinburgh run, the car would be taken to Brooklands racetrack and run flat out.

The Napier came through the test with an enviable record. Top gear performance was excellent, the car attained a 19.35 miles-per-gallon fuel consumption record, and achieved a maximum speed of 76.42 miles per hour at Brooklands.

The men at Rolls-Royce determined right away to meet this challenge. Claude Johnson sought, and got, permission from the R.A.C. to put a Silver Ghost through the same London-to-Edinburgh run. A special car was built for the run. It was unlike any previous Rolls-Royce.

Chassis number 1701 E was selected to prove once and for all that Rolls-Royce was the best car in the world. A lightweight body was fitted to the chassis, and fitted is really the word, since the body was no wider than the chassis width of 3 feet. It was so narrow that a small projection had to be made in the body to accommodate the driver's foot on the accelerator. The bonnet swept up to meet the rest of the body, rendering obsolete the straight-bonnet-to-vertical-scuttle designs which had been standard to that time. The rear springing was changed from the standard three-quarter elliptical springs to cantilevered rear springs. The engine output was increased by fitting a larger carburetor and increasing the compression ratio. Top gear ratio was 2.9:1. In actual size and in output, the Rolls-Royce was smaller than the record-setting Napier.

In September of 1911 the car was ready. It was a beautiful sports car for that era, and remains one of the outstanding Rolls-Royce designs to this day. The driver chosen for the event was E. W. Hives, a tester for the company since 1908. As you can imagine, with a 3-foot width, there was barely room for Hives and his three passengers to sit side by side. On September 6 they all squeezed in and took off.

On September 13 it was all over for Napier. The Silver Ghost had taken the top-gear-only run in stride easily, recording 24.32 miles per gallon of fuel consumed, and hitting a maximum speed of 78.26 at Brooklands. Claude Johnson, Henry Royce, and E. W. Hives had good reason to be happy after their performance. They had another reason to be happy. The design of the London-to-Edinburgh car caught on so well that the company decided to produce replicas for interested buyers. The car in this painting is one of the first of these replicas.

A ridiculous controversy followed the Rolls-Royce success, with barbs flying back and forth between the Napier and Rolls-Royce works. Napier claimed that the Silver Ghost had a special wind-cheating radiator, which was nonsense since the car had the traditional Rolls-Royce radiator design which is anything but streamlined. Napier also claimed that the Hives car only carried three people while the Napier had carried four. Claude Johnson countered that by stating that the fourth passenger had crouched forward to cut down wind resistance. And since the whole run had been observed by the R.A.C., it was all a little absurd to argue about it.

The wind resistance bit did give Johnson an idea, however. He prepared a London–Edinburgh chassis with a streamlined single-seat aluminum body and sent it to Brooklands to see what it would do. The car covered the flying half mile at 101.8 miles per hour. Quite a speed for 1911. To top it off, this same car could travel in top gear at a man's walking pace with no hint of stall or vibration!

The painter has placed this beautiful L-E Ghost at rest by a wheat field in Scotland. The plaid is made from the tartan of the royal house of Stewart. The small photograph shows the first Silver Ghost in the Scottish Reliability Trial of 1907, the competition which began the legend of the Silver Ghost. The advertisement is painted from *The Autocar* of February 4, 1905, and indicated the good press that the new Rolls-Royce motorcars were getting at that time.

What of the driver Hives? His success became as well known as that of the car he drove. He later became Lord Hives, and in 1946 became managing director of Rolls-Royce, Ltd., taking the company through the tough postwar years with great skill. He died in 1965 at the age of seventy-nine.

Melbourne Brindle

THE PRIDE
OF A MAHARAJAH 1911

Car collectors as a group are a mixed bag. Some have two cars, others have hundreds. Some spend thousands and thousands of dollars to restore each new acquisition; others store their antique hulks for years in conditions that rot the cars faster than being out in the weather. Some specialize in a particular marque because they love it, others because it is the thing to do. Some meet visitors with shotguns, others make their collections available to all comers. Often their obsession (read hobby) benefits the rest of us who are able to visit their collections or museums and wish. . . .

Elsewhere in this book we have seen how the Rolls-Royce Silver Ghost was introduced to India, and the way maharajahs began their contemporary collections of the cars. Actually, it is only with our hindsight and present collecting boom that we can call these accumulations of Rolls-Royce cars "collections." The maharajahs just bought cars to have them around and use them. Every morning one could play "eeny, meeny, miny, moe" with up to fifty Rolls-Royce cars. Nice game if you could afford it.

The Maharajah of Mysore could afford it. As ruler of a large southern Indian state, he was a very wealthy man who could call his own shots. Yet events that took place before he was born almost deprived him of his wealth and his title.

The Maharajah's grandfather had been placed on his throne as a child by the British. In 1810 this Maharajah took over the governing of the state. Twenty years of poor administration on his part led to insurrection; so the British took over the government and set the Maharajah aside. The state became a model province of British India.

In 1861 the Maharajah asked for restoration of his kingdom, but was turned down. He was an old man and had no heir, so the British decided that the state would be better off without him. The Maharajah persisted, however, and in 1865 he adopted an infant son. After much political maneuvering it was decided in 1867 that this heir could succeed his adoptive father when he came of age.

The young man was raised in the English manner, with English tutors and a thorough European education. In 1881 at the age of eighteen he was installed as Maharajah Chamaranjendra in accordance with his agreement with the British. Chamaranjendra died in 1894, leaving a son to succeed him, Maharajah Sri Krishnarajah Wadiyar.

In 1902 the young Maharajah of Mysore was vested with full powers. He was one of the richest men in the world. His reign was to see many exciting changes in India.

The Maharajah of Mysore added this Rolls-Royce Silver Ghost to his stable in 1911. That was the same year King George V and Queen Mary came to the Delhi Durbar, the Indian confirmation of their Majesties' coronation.

An Imperial Camp was formed in Delhi which covered 25 square miles. Over a third of a million people resided there in nearly 50,000 tents. The amphitheatre in which the royal reception took place held 12,000 people and 18,000 troops, all facing the two silver thrones. One by one the Princes of India paid homage to their sovereigns —among them, the ruler of Mysore.

This Silver Ghost throne-on-wheels was reputed to be the favorite motorcar of the Maharajah, and as such was reserved for state occasions. It is not difficult to imagine him motoring away from his multistoried palace with his turbaned driver at the wheel and liveried attendants standing up behind the high victoria top.

The car has a wheelbase of 143½ inches, yet looks much longer, perhaps because it has no windscreen to break the expanse from front mudguard tips to the victoria top. It certainly must have been a magnificent sight as the Maharajah was transported through the streets of his kingdom.

The Maharajah died in 1940 after a long and fruitful reign. His car somehow found its way back to England after World War II. There it was completely restored and then sold at auction.

An American collector, Mr. James C. Leake of Muskogee, Oklahoma, was the highest bidder and paid $27,000 for the car. It was shipped to Oklahoma where it joined Mr. Leake's collection of more than seventy automobiles, including many other examples of Rolls-Royce craftsmanship.

The painter has placed this motorcar in the courtyard of India's most beautiful building, the Taj Mahal. The silver plaque is from this car and bears the chassis number 1683. The Spirit of Ecstasy mascot was designed by sculptor Charles Sykes the same year this Ghost was built.

Built for a man who bought expensive automobiles the way most men buy pipes, or women buy hats, this car has indeed enjoyed an unusual career. It has passed from the State of Mysore to the State of Oklahoma, leaving one collection to join another. The car has traveled only 9,000 miles under its own power. It has traveled many more miles than that by sea.

ROLLS-ROYCE LTD
LONDON & DERBY
N.º 1663

Melbourne Brindle

HOOPER LIMOUSINE 1911

The collecting and restoring of old cars is more than a hobby. It can get to be a way of living in that it colors every aspect of the enthusiast's life. Social events are opportunities to meet new people who may know of old cars in their areas. Weekends are spent at old car meets, or out "beating the bush" to find cars. Driveways and garages are littered with dilapidated hulks and the smell of kerosene and raw gasoline. Neighbors become accustomed to a constant traffic of towed antiques (rusty junk, no doubt, to them) and friends of the enthusiast who visit at all hours to talk or help.

Every old car buff, however wealthy or however poor he may be, nurtures the dream that each barn or field he sees holds a potential dream car. Riding down a country lane with one of these types can be an eye-opening experience, because a car hunter has become adept at recognizing a car from abandoned parts which rise above high grass in a field. He can somehow see "something interesting" through a 6-inch gap between boards in a barn. A glimpse of reflected sunlight off a fallen headlight is enough to cause a screeching of brakes and a bold inquiry at the nearby farmhouse. Most often the spotted item turns out to be part of a tractor or an undesirable car—but there's always the chance that it might be something else again.

Car hunters have become experts with innovative ploys to get information about cars: one stroke of pure genius was mass-mailing queries to rural postmasters to ask if mail carriers knew of cars on their routes.

The unknown enthusiast reportedly had great success with the technique, but made the mistake of telling friends about it. Soon, a lot of rural post offices were receiving more mail from car buffs than they were for residents, and the practice ended.

Many of the finds, true or not, have become legendary. Two of these come to mind, because they have been heard in so many different forms. The first involves a lucky (and always nameless) fellow who got a tip that the widow of a recently deceased actor (name any recently deceased actor) wanted to sell his prized car (Mercedes SSK, Type 57 Bugatti, Duesenberg, etc.). The car nut arrives at the house, is met by the bereft widow, and led to a garage. There sits the beautiful car. She explains that the sight of it brings back so many memories of her late husband that she wants to get rid of it. The enthusiast, who in all the versions is a young man who can get hold of about $350 in one lump, asks the price and is told $250 or some such ridiculous price. Naturally, he grabs the deal, and drives off into the night with the deal of a lifetime.

The second is the story of a little old lady in Denver (or San Francisco, or Seattle) who loves Model T Fords. In 1927 she hears that Henry Ford will stop making the Model T. Aghast, she orders three, planning to drive the first until it wears out, and then replace it with the second, and so on. Of course, she dies before cars two and three can be used, and they sit in storage in crates until years pass and a local car buff buys them up for a song. Two brand new Model Ts! Yes, the shaggy-car stories go on and on.

68

Many car enthusiasts take a direct approach and advertise in newspapers for old cars. In the case of this Hooper limousine, the advertiser not only got a response, but a car in an old barn as well. And what an old car it was.

In 1945 Mr. S. J. Skinner, who was not yet the owner of the Barker flush-side torpedo shown elsewhere in this book, advertised in the London *Times* for a car. A response came from the daughter of Lord Wavetree. There was an old car of her father's out in the barn, and would Mr. Skinner be interested?

Mr. Skinner, it turned out, was not interested, as he was earnestly searching for a touring car. But he put Mr. Stanley Sears in touch with Lord Wavetree's daughter. Mr. Sears traveled to Wheatly, in Oxfordshire, where he found the Silver Ghost Hooper limousine, chassis number 1721, inhabited by several hens, eggs, and chicken droppings.

With Mr. Skinner's help, the chicken coop on wheels was towed to the station for shipment. Restoration was begun immediately and resulted in the beautiful brass-bound motorcar seen here.

Along with the car, Mr. Sears inherited a fascinating but unauthenticated story. The story was that the car had reportedly been ordered by King George V. Once it was completed, King George decided that perhaps he had better stick to Daimlers. So the car was purchased by a Mr. Walker. In 1919, a barony was created for Mr. Walker and he became Lord Wavetree.

Between 1912 and his death in 1933, Lord Wavetree amassed a total of 230,000 miles on his limousine. After his death, the car was put away in the barn and almost forgotten for twelve years until the advertisement in *The Times* brought it to the motorhouse of Mr. Sears, where it resides with several other immaculate examples of Rolls-Royce craftsmanship.

To be sure, all this occurred in 1945, before the big car-collecting boom had begun, but the moral of this story is that car buffs should never think that all the wonderful old cars have been rooted out. There may be a Silver Ghost in that very next barn.

HOOPER & Co. Ltd.
MOTOR-BODY-BUILDERS
TO

HIS MAJESTY THE KING
HER MAJESTY THE QUEEN
HER MAJESTY QUEEN ALEXANDRA
H·I·M· THE GERMAN EMPEROR

ROLLS-RO
LONDON &
Nº 172

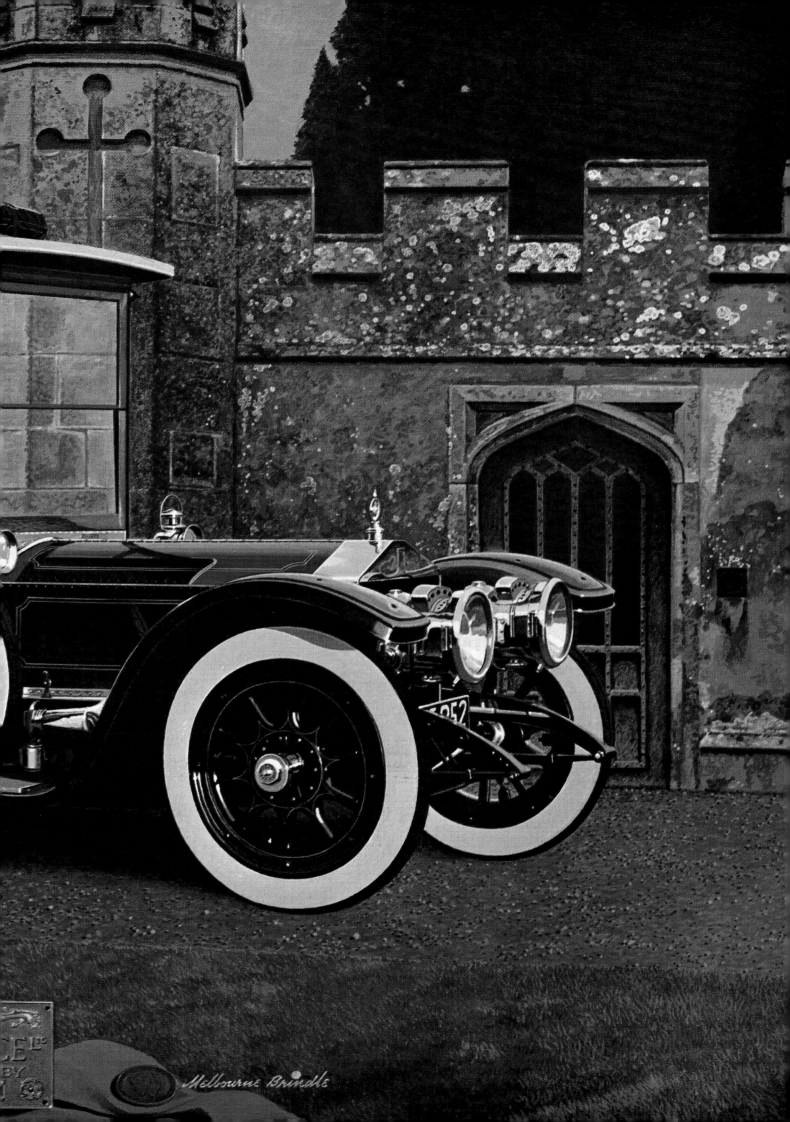

Melbourne Brindle

TORPEDO-PHAETON— LONDON–EDINBURGH 1913

Depending on how involved you are with automobiles, you have several alternatives open when you go to buy a new car. Perhaps you buy a particular make because you've always bought it, or because your father did. Maybe you've believed the advertising for a certain car and decided to give it a whirl. Then there's the recommendation of your neighbor. But most often, people rely on the motoring press to give reliable evaluations of new cars in road tests.

Whether you read the all-out enthusiasts' magazines or *Consumer Reports*, you're trying to discover the advantages of one car over another, or trying to see just what the model you had in mind will do flat out.

The motoring press had a great influence in the early 1900s also. Almost as soon as there were motorcars, there were books and magazines about how to buy, handle, and care for them. As is the case today, the people who put the publications out for sale in those pioneering days were dyed-in-the-wool enthusiasts. While a motoring journalist might prefer a particular make of car over another, he seldom really damned one outright in his writings. He properly phrased things to let you know that a certain car had much better hill-climbing ability than another—although the other car had many other good points.

In 1911 the original London–Edinburgh Silver Ghost had once again proved the supremacy of the Rolls-Royce motorcars. The feat, which is described elsewhere in this book, gained some very good press for the company, and it decided to produce the L-E chassis for interested customers.

In 1913, a representative of *The Autocar* got into a lively discussion with Mr. Percy W. Northey at the Royal Automobile Club. Mr. Northey was a driver of some worth, and was employed by Rolls-Royce. His first success with the marque had been his noteworthy second place in the 1905 Tourist Trophy race driving the then unknown Rolls-Royce motorcar.

The *Autocar* writer had owned or driven a great many motorcars, some with three-speed gearboxes and others with four-speed gearing. It was his opinion that a gearbox with a top fourth gear was best in a motorcar, since the drop in ratio from a top third gear into second speed was too great to allow smooth running. Mr. Northey did not agree and volunteered to prove his point in a trip through the hills of Kent and Surrey in a 1913 L-E type with the standard Silver Ghost three-speed gearbox.

The man from *Autocar* chose the route, and Northey was to do the driving. It was to be the motoring journalist's second Rolls-Royce experience—the first having been a 100-mile trip in the first Silver Ghost which led to the praise quoted in the text about that car in this book. He was to be equally impressed with this Ghost.

"The car seems to be neither drawn nor thrust, but actually seduced away," he wrote in an *Autocar* report of the trip. His route purposely included a number of hills designed to test the gearing of the car. The first of these was a slope on which most medium-powered cars of the day were required to downshift in two separate places. The Ghost stayed in top gear and ". . . just rolled it out behind it like a machine delivering tape."

The next two slopes, Titsey and Westerham Hills, were taken with smooth shifts to second speed. The speed dropped very little as the Ghost swept smoothly upward. These were hills which the journalist said would have appalled motorists seven to ten years earlier.

When the trip was over, the *Autocar* writer was still firm in his conviction that the average car performed better with four speeds, but went on, ". . . we should be unfair to the Rolls-Royce if we did not admit that four speeds would have been superfluous upon the distinctly hilly run we undertook, and would have necessitated at least two additional gear changes in covering the stiff route we selected, and that without any corresponding advantage." At the article's end, one is left with the impression that the writer considered the L-E Ghost quite a superior motorcar.

The London–Edinburgh Silver Ghost in this painting is an identical twin to the car reported on in *The Autocar*. In fact, it is the same car photographed to illustrate the 1913 article in that magazine.

On the earlier L-E type portrayed in this book, the newly devised cantilevered rear springs ride under the axle. On this car, and L-E models with chassis numbers above 1994, the springs are over the axle. The latter springing was adopted for all Silver Ghosts after chassis number 2100. The springs slid in trunnions on these newer versions.

Early cars required much more maintenance than cars do today. For example, the cantilevered rear springs required oiling every 250 miles, or "weekly" according to Rolls-Royce maintenance schedules. Just about every moving part had an oil cup which was to be used according to the book. Careful attention to this procedure surely helped add to the running life of many a Rolls-Royce car.

Barker, Cann, and Midland Counties Garage all supplied coachwork along "sporting lines" for London–Edinburgh cars. This one is fitted with Rudge-Whitworth wire wheels to complete the sporting look.

The small painting seemingly paper-clipped on depicts a driver's eye view of the pedals and instruments on a Ghost. The setting for the large painting was inspired by a visit by the artist to the home of Eustace and Joan Wade at Sharsted in Kent. Their daughter, Virginia Wade, who practiced faithfully on this grass court, won the tennis championship for England at Forest Hills, New York, in 1969. This is the painter's tribute to her.

Melbourne Brindle

THE CONTINENTAL-"ALPINE EAGLE" 1913

Fine automobiles have a "thing" all their own—a charisma which is often unassociated with the people who own and drive them. Yet, every so often a person or a group of people becomes so associated with a make or model that one seldom hears of one without the other. Such was the case with the notorious Bentley Boys who won fame with their exploits in Bentley race cars in the late 1920s and early 1930s. And such was the case with James Radley, whose name became synonymous with famous Rolls-Royce Silver Ghost Continental motorcars.

Radley was the Continental's raison d'être, since it was built to overcome an unfortunate situation he had caused.

Radley did not work for Rolls-Royce. He owned a London–Edinburgh model and competed with it very successfully—until the 1912 Austrian Alpine Trials.

During that competition, Radley's Ghost failed to climb the Katschberg Pass. The car just stopped, unable to go on until two passengers had stepped out. This kind of behavior was, heretofore, unheard of by Rolls-Royce cars. Things like that just didn't happen. It was a disgrace. Radley was unhappy about the whole thing, but Henry Royce and Claude Johnson were stunned and shocked. The episode made the motoring press soon after, and Johnson and Royce set about ensuring that nothing like that would *ever* happen again.

After a stint of testing on the continent, Rolls-Royce created a new model of Silver Ghost called the Continental. The car had improved suspension, increased cooling capacity, more horsepower, and, most important, a new four-speed gearbox with a low gear that would pull the car over just about anything.

When the 1913 Austrian Alpine Trials were announced, Rolls-Royce was ready with a team of three Continental models. Radley backed up this team with his private Continental, chassis number 2260E, the car in this painting. The idea was not only to win the competition, but to win so decisively that the disgrace of the previous year would be wiped out.

Rules of the trial required that bonnets and radiators be sealed so that no mechanical adjustments could be made, and no water added. (This may have been the origin of the legend that all Rolls-Royce cars were sold with lifetime guarantees and sealed bonnets to insure no tinkering by owners.) Each of the Rolls-Royce entrants had an extension fitted to the radiator filler neck to relieve cooling pressures.

Early in June, 1913, the four beautiful cars left on the journey to Vienna to start the trial. The three team cars traveled together on the dusty French roads, but Radley . . . Radley was a robust man of tremendous endurance and courage. He never liked to be anywhere but out front in anything he did. His mechanic on the trip was a Rolls-Royce tester named Ward. Ward wrote home about the 500 miles that Radley drove from Paris to Turin in one stint.

Radley was anxious to prove the worth of his car. One evening in Vienna before the trial began, his companions bet him 1,000 crowns that he could not drive to Klagenfurt and back between sunrise and sunset. It was a mere 400 miles—short work for Radley—so he took the bet and suggested that everyone stay up the remainder of the night to see him off at sunrise.

Three passengers accompanied him, and they returned in thirteen hours to win the bet. Had they stopped at all? Oh, yes, for breakfast, lunch, and for an hour or so when one of the passengers got ill and needed to rest!

When Loibl, one of the most difficult passes, was reached, Radley slowed down at the base until he had the road to himself. Then he planted his foot flat on the floor and roared upwards. He tossed his car around the numerous hairpin turns with abandon. The best previous time for the ascent was eight and one-half minutes. Radley made it in five.

Radley and two team cars finished one, two, three. The third team car had been in an accident which locked it in third gear. It finished but kept the Rolls-Royce team from winning the team prize.

They had won the event, though, and won it in such a fashion that the prestige of Rolls-Royce cars was once again the highest.

When the Austrian event was announced in 1914, Rolls-Royce decided to rest on its laurels and give others a chance. Radley didn't see it that way. Once again he entered his personal Ghost. This time he upheld the Rolls-Royce tradition alone.

The first day Radley succeeded in passing the four larger cars ahead of him to come in first by forty-two minutes. The second day he raced a Benz for many miles, only to discover that his speed had taken them past a fork before the flag marshals had come on the scene to direct him properly. He and the Benz were 45 miles off course. When he got back on course, fifty-four cars had gone ahead of him. He passed all but two before the next stopping point.

The next couple of days were a breeze for Radley. He took the passes in stride until Innsbruck was reached. Here the competitors were to rest for a day. But Radley heard of a new pass, Turracherhohe, that had been added to the trial and wanted to see it himself. It was supposedly impassable by motorcar. His own car was impounded for the night, so he borrowed a sister car from a friend and set off alone on the 250 miles to the pass. He was gone all the following day, and by nightfall, Ward, again his mechanic on this trial, began to fear for him. The competition was due to start at 4:45 A.M. in the morning and at 4:00 A.M. Radley still hadn't appeared. At 4:30 Radley appeared looking hardly worn from his 500-mile trip. Ward hopped in the borrowed car and they motored to the car park to get his own for the day's competition.

Radley drove the entire day, including climbing Turracherhohe, after having no sleep for two nights and driving almost continuously for three days and two nights.

Out of seventy-eight starters in the trial that year, fourteen did not lose marks. Radley was one of them in the only British car to do so. By virtue of his performance in the two timed events he could easily say his was the finest performance in the event.

Following the success of Rolls-Royce cars in these two trials, the Continental model was renamed the Alpine Eagle. The car shown here is the only remaining one of the four which competed in the 1913 trial.

THE ROUTE OF THE 1913 AUSTRIAN ALPINE TRIAL
"The Autocar"

dley completed the first 260 miles of the course
ht hours. The other Rolls-Royces came in next,
quarters of an hour later, followed by the
va team, who, as events subsequently showed
the only ones who came within measurable
ce of holding the English cars in speed.
ely over the top, however, we glided down to
g and Mautendorf, and then at St Michael-in-
au faced the violently quick rise on to the Katsch
oad. The surface proved to be rougher than
ear, in contrast to the Tauern Road, which is
ved; and what made matters worse was that
oughest parts were at the steepest points.
he Rolls-Royce cars went up on half throttle
onsummate ease. Radley tells me that his average
was over twenty-five miles an hour, and that
the final precipitous stretch he did not fall
seventeen miles an hour.
Broccone Pass the Rolls-Royces came past in
style, and I am bound to say that I have never
anything more beautiful in the way of locomotion
he way in which they flew up the pass. It was a
acle indeed worth going many a long mile to see,
could wish that we had a similar testing ground
gland. Beautiful in another way, moreover, was the
, described to me later by a spectator who
d down upon the cars rising to the summit of
Pass (7,382 feet) where he was stationed; as
rounded one bend after another, spread o
forty yards apart, the Rolls-Royces seemed to be
iving embodiment of grace and power.

Melbourne Brindle

A YELLOW ROLLS-ROYCE TWO-SEATER PHAETON 1914

There are few places in the world today where an automobile is not looked on as a necessity. True, many people living in urban centers such as New York City do not feel the need of a car because of convenient mass transit facilities. But for the rest of us, our ignition key is as important as our house key, and we take the reliability of our cars and roads very much for granted.

Many readers will remember when that wasn't so. If we take the year 1900 as a round figure for the beginning of popular motoring, then it took nearly fifty years to develop a nationwide highway system that was adequate for the number of vehicles available to use it. In many ways our highways are still far behind in coping with the millions of cars owned by Americans.

Driving is not an adventure anymore for the vast majority of people. It is a means to an end. We pull onto our superhighways, set our speedometers on a certain speed and whiz along, listening to the radio and watching the outdoor advertising boards fly by. Scenery is forgotten; weather is seldom important; only the traffic counts, and the time. We eat at drive-ins which specialize in feeding motorized millions as quickly as possible. If our vehicle experiences trouble, we wait for a professional to come by with his truck and repair whatever is wrong. Many of us won't even change a flat tire— or don't know how.

Most drivers from our affluent age wouldn't have made it past their garage doors in the pre–World War I motoring days. Imagine, if you will, that it is 1914, and you are fortunate enough to own this beautiful Rolls-Royce Silver Ghost phaeton. It is a lovely spring day and you and your lady decide to go for a ride. It is the chauffeur's day off. First you check to see that you have gasoline, and add some by pouring it from a container, through a chamois strainer, into a funnel to the gas tank. The oil is next, and it is topped up from the oil container on the shelf of the motorshed. Is the repair kit in the storage compartment? It is, containing all the important tools for repairing the car on the road—especially the tire patch kit and tire pump.

It is time to start the motor. First you set the fuel mixture control to give a richer mixture. Now move the ignition lever on the right side of the steering quadrant toward "Early" to advance the spark. Move the left lever which controls the manual throttle toward "Fast." Proceed to the front of the car and grasp the starting handle, and turn the engine over two or three times to ensure that the cylinders have gasoline. Return to the driver's compartment and turn the ignition-control knob in the center of the quadrant to position "B"—for battery. Return to the front of the car and, taking care to tuck your thumb under the crank (to avoid breaking it or your arm in case of backfire), give one hefty pull upward. With this Rolls-Royce that's usually all it takes to get the engine running. Then return to the steering wheel and adjust all the levers to give the engine a smooth idle and a proper gasoline mixture. Switch the knob over to magneto and the Bosch unit will take over the ignition function.

Now your lady is ready. She has a large wicker picnic hamper prepared with all the things you love to eat. You help her in, climb in yourself, and you're off.

Your speed is quite low as you journey smoothly along. In the United States the roads are still dirt or gravel for the most part (England has better roads paved with bitumen, a form of asphalt), and you leave a lot of dust in your wake. Soon you are in unfamiliar territory, and the road signs are no help at all, being placed mainly for the convenience of people living in the surrounding area. After inquiring at the hardware store where you buy more gasoline, you continue your journey in the right direction.

Stopping to eat is the major event of the afternoon. The car is pulled off the road onto some grassy spot. Your lady spreads a cloth on the ground and you eat heartily, taking an hour or so to do it. After eating you lie back on the grass for a midday nap —good for the digestion, you know. `

A drop of rain awakens you. Your lady hurriedly gathers the eating materials while you struggle to raise the black leather hood. In spite of the manufacturer's claims, this hood-raising takes some time and you are getting soaked as the rain increases.

Finally you have it raised and get in the car. Since the engine is now cold, all the starting procedures must be repeated, making it necessary for you to get out of the car a couple of times.

Off you drive, with the rain coming in through the open sides because you've left the side curtains at home. There are no windshield wipers, so your view is distorted. You drive hurriedly now, trying to get home as quickly as possible.

Suddenly you hear a muffled bang. A flat tire brings you to a halt in the muddy road. Rolls-Royce has refined practically everything on your car, but it still has no control over the tires or the horseshoe nails that are in the road by the thousands.

You change the tire, after locating a sturdy board to keep the jack from sinking in the mud. Thank heavens for the Dunlop detachable wire wheels that let you change the tire more quickly. Dripping wet and covered with mud you return to the car and pull away, having remembered to leave the engine running while the tire was being changed.

Hours later, after entering mudholes so deep that the wire wheels look as though they were solid brown metal, you make it home. Quite an adventure. It may take the chauffeur days to clean the car, but he'll get it spotless before the next trip.

Certainly not all motorcar journeys had this ending. Most were worse. The owner of a Rolls-Royce had one big thing going for him, and that was the reliability of his car. Pity the motorist who bought another make which was not reliable. No wonder the song, "Get Out and Get Under" was so popular.

Almost nothing is known of the Silver Ghost in this painting. *The Autocar* of December 12, 1914, carried a picture of it, without telling the chassis number or owner. The beautifully proportioned body was built by Mann, Egerton & Co., Ltd. It has disappeared without a trace, leaving only the memory of what it must have been like to drive such a magnificent vehicle in those early days of motoring.

D., NORWICH & LONDON

Melbourne Brindle

SILVER GHOST USED BY KING GEORGE V 1914

By 1914 the motorcar was established. No longer rich men's toys, motorcars were a fact of life—everyday life—in America, in Great Britain, and on the Continent. When World War I broke out in Europe, it was only natural to turn this newest convenience into the newest tool of war.

In the case of the Rolls-Royce armored cars, described elsewhere in this book, the automobile became a weapon. But many Rolls-Royce touring cars and limousines became logistic necessities and proved worthy under the most arduous conditions.

Right from the start of the war, Sir John French, Commander in Chief of British Forces, had chosen a Rolls-Royce Silver Ghost as his staff car. So did Field Marshal Sir Douglas Haig, General Snow, General Seeley, Brigadier General Sadiler-Jackson, Secretary of State for War Lord Kitchener, French War Minister M. Millerand, French General Gourand, General Allenby, and many others.

Lord Kitchener's car was given to him by the company when the war broke out. After Kitchener's death on a British cruiser which struck a mine, Lloyd George took his job at the War Office and inherited the car with the job. When Lloyd George became Prime Minister, he brought the Ghost along. After leaving office he bought the car and kept it in service for many years. Finally it was offered to the Imperial War Museum, which declined, and so the car was broken up by a junk yard. Only the radiator was kept as a souvenir.

Often when cars were donated to the war effort the owners came along with them. This was the case with the Royal Automobile Club Corps. Twenty-five well-to-do adventurers volunteered to drive their cars wherever they were needed. Several were Rolls-Royce owners. James Radley, intrepid winner of the 1913 and 1914 Austrian Alpine Trials, was one. The Duke of Westminster, who later gained fame in Rolls-Royce armored cars, was another. Their first task was to get General Snow and his staff from Le Havre to Sir John French's headquarters. General Snow was bringing a division of troops to try to halt the British retreat from Mons. Radley and company fairly flew across France, depositing General Snow at Sir John French's side faster than would normally have been possible.

After that, Radley drove General Snow everywhere. Once the General wanted to visit a spot very close to the enemy. Radley parked in a sunken road while the General reconnoitered on foot. Some time had gone by when suddenly retreating British soldiers jumped into the sunken lane and set up a machine gun. Radley asked if they had seen the General. They had; he had gone over to the right of the line. The soldiers suggested that Radley get out—if he could.

Once out of the protection of the sunken road, the bullets flew around Radley's Rolls. He went flat out to the rear, to find out later that the General had forgotten him.

Baron Rothschild gave up his Ghost to an army driver, then learned to drive and took over as driver himself. The car fell into enemy hands when the Baron, whose expertise did not match his zeal, crashed the car into a pole in the face of the advancing Germans. The Baron couldn't bear to let his car be captured, so he carefully removed all the instruments and hammered the engine into scrap before escaping on foot.

In reply to an urgent request from the War Office, the secretary of the R.A.C. set up the King's Messenger Service in September, 1914. Four Rolls-Royce Ghosts and drivers were directed to maintain a constant service between French ports and British General Headquarters at Villeneuve St. George. A Ghost carrying dispatches started from each end of the route every day.

The service continued for two years, with the position of GHQ changing many times during that period. Yet, the Rolls-Royce cars never suffered a breakdown. In fact, it got so that people along the route set their clocks by the Rolls-Royce of the King's Messenger Service.

These feats of reliability were common to Rolls-Royce motorcars during the war. Harold Nockolds tells of many grueling wartime Rolls-Royce heroics in his book, *The Magic of a Name*. One car was being dismantled by the Duchess of Cazes as the Germans advanced toward the Marne. She was alone and did not want her husband's car in German hands. Along came a British officer and she gave the car to him. The car had 25,000 miles on it then and had never had an overhaul. The officer put another 25,000 miles on the odometer in sixteen months, yet the car required no maintenance other than relining the hand brake.

Another Ghost, driven by a Frenchman attached to a British Cavalry regiment, covered 18,000 miles of field-and-stream driving in five months. It stopped only once involuntarily, because of a bit of dirt in the carburetor air valve.

The French War Minister had one Silver Ghost, then ordered two more. The two new ones each went some 20,000 miles in three months through woods, over fields and the like. General Gourand's Rolls-Royce went 60,000 battlefront miles without a repair.

When King George visited the battlegrounds he always traveled with a fleet of Rolls-Royce cars. This car is the one that carried the King and the Prince of Wales during their 1916 inspection of France and Belgium. The car is a 1914 model, built on an Alpine Silver Ghost chassis. The royal insignia on the radiator and the flag on the roof let everyone know whose limousine this was.

The Prince of Wales (later King Edward VIII and still later Duke of Windsor) had one rather unfortunate experience in a Rolls-Royce during one of his visits. He and a fellow officer had been driven to a town that was under shellfire twenty-four hours a day by the Germans. Leaving the car, the Prince and his companion walked forward toward the front lines. Suddenly, a shell exploded to the rear of them. Running back they discovered that a piece of shrapnel had crashed through the windshield of their car and killed the driver instantly. The Prince knew how to drive and took the dead driver to a casualty station, then completed his tour of the front. A month or so later the Prince had that car's body removed and sent to Derby, where it was fitted to the first Rolls-Royce owned by him.

When the war became a trench stalemate, the widespread, cross-country use of staff cars slowed quite a bit, but Rolls-Royce cars continued to remain in high favor and added to their reputation as the best cars in the world.

IN THIS ROLLS-ROYCE SILVER GHOST,
& THE PRINCE OF WALES, VISITED EU

MAJESTY KING GEORGE V.
...PE DURING WORLD WAR 1

Melbourne Brindle

EMPRESS MARIE'S LANDAULET 1914

In another part of this book the reader will learn of the Rolls-Royce Silver Ghost of Prince Yusupov of Russia and the part it may have played in the murder of Rasputin, which in turn may have led to the murder of Czar Nicholas II and members of his family by Russian revolutionists.

One of the survivors of the royal murders was Dowager Empress Marie, mother of Czar Nicholas II and widow of Czar Alexander III. Her unusual story is a mixture of sadness and happiness and shows the heights and depths of royal life.

Born Princess Dagmar of Denmark, Marie was a sister of Princess Alexandra, who married Edward, Prince of Wales, and became Queen of England. Princess Dagmar was originally engaged to Czarevich Nicholas, son of Czar Alexander II of Russia. When Nicholas died, he left his title of Czarevich and his fiancée, Princess Dagmar, to his brother Alexander. To understand this, we must remember that we are speaking of the age of absolute monarchy, when a king, or czar, had absolute control over every one of his subjects. Apparently some of his power rubbed off on the Czar-to-be as well.

As a gesture of goodwill to Russia, Princess Dagmar took the name Marie Fedorovna before marrying Alexander. She soon became Czarina, or Empress, Marie, when two terrorists' bombs led to the death of Alexander II, on March 13, 1881, and her husband became Czar Alexander III.

Alexander III was a gigantic man, standing 6 feet 4 inches. He was like a big Russian bear, dominating everything with which he came in contact. He led a Spartan personal life, and was thoroughly dedicated to his job of absolute control over every living thing, every inch of ground, and every drop of water that was in Russia. He dressed in peasant clothes in private life, not caring that they were threadbare. His children slept on army cots, bathed each morning in cold water, and ate rough food.

The public life of the Czar was another thing entirely. Russia at the time of Czar Alexander III was still striving for the Westernization which had begun under the rule of Peter the Great, some two centuries before.

The language of the wealthy was French, not Russian. Jewels were very much in fashion and very much in evidence. A continuous round of events was planned and well-attended by those who could afford it. Members of the royal family were expected to partake in these social events, and did.

By 1894, the strain of the immense job of ruling an emerging country and carrying on an active social life brought about the death of Alexander III. His son Nicholas II inherited the throne, but had not received proper training for his position. Alexander III had only been forty-nine years old when he died, and probably felt that there was plenty of time to teach young Nicholas how to rule. Nicholas himself felt his own failings and dreaded the power which was now his.

Now the Dowager Empress, Marie was reluctant to give up the life she had led as Czarina. She continued to treat her son, the Czar, like a child, much to the displeasure of Czarina Alexandra, wife of Nicholas II. A typical example was the episode of the crown jewels.

Marie was very fond of jewels, and some of the crown jewels were traditionally passed on from empress to empress. In fact, it was almost required that the jewels be worn by the empress on many occasions. Nicholas asked his mother to turn the jewels over to Alexandra and was refused. Alexandra, in a huff, declared that she didn't want them anyway, but the scandal never became public because Marie eventually handed them over.

Rolls-Royce Silver Ghosts were jewels of another kind to Russian nobility. Czar Nicholas II had two; we know of one belonging to Prince Yusupov; and Dowager Empress Marie had this beautiful landaulet. It is pictured outside the Ekaterininsky Palace. Note the two-headed Imperial Russian Eagle, symbol of the power of the Romanov Czars, worked into the ironwork on the balcony. The small brooch is a painted miniature of Peter the Great. The broken string of pearls symbolizes Dowager Empress Marie's flight from Russia during the revolution which destroyed much of her family and destroyed life as she knew it in Russia.

On July 16, 1918, deposed Czar Nicholas and his family were murdered by Bolsheviks. Empress Marie was in the Crimea and heard rumors of the killings but refused to believe them. In April of 1919, when the Red Army made advances in the Crimea, Marie was persuaded to leave Russia by her sister, Queen Mother Alexandra of England, and her nephew King George V. She left on board a British battleship sent for her.

Dowager Empress Marie went back to her Danish homeland to live in a wing of the royal palace. Her nephew, King Christian of Denmark, did not like her very much, and the feeling was mutual. He tried to get her to sell some of the jewels she had brought with her to pay some of her expenses. She refused. Her financial problems were solved when King George of England provided her with £10,000 a year.

Empress Marie never admitted that she believed that her son, the Czar, was murdered. She never met any of the pretenders who claimed to be her granddaughter, Anastasia, which is unfortunate, as her identification could possibly have ended the mystery which continues today.

In 1928, at the age of eighty-one, Dowager Empress Marie died. Her Rolls-Royce Silver Ghost has disappeared without trace. In a small way, however, another Rolls-Royce Silver Ghost shows the irony of the Russian Revolution.

The Bolsheviks wanted to make all men equal in Russia and eliminate the wealthy classes—the people who could afford such things as Rolls-Royce motorcars. Yet, a 1919 Rolls-Royce Silver Ghost, chassis number 16X, is on display in Moscow today. Its owner was a man named Lenin.

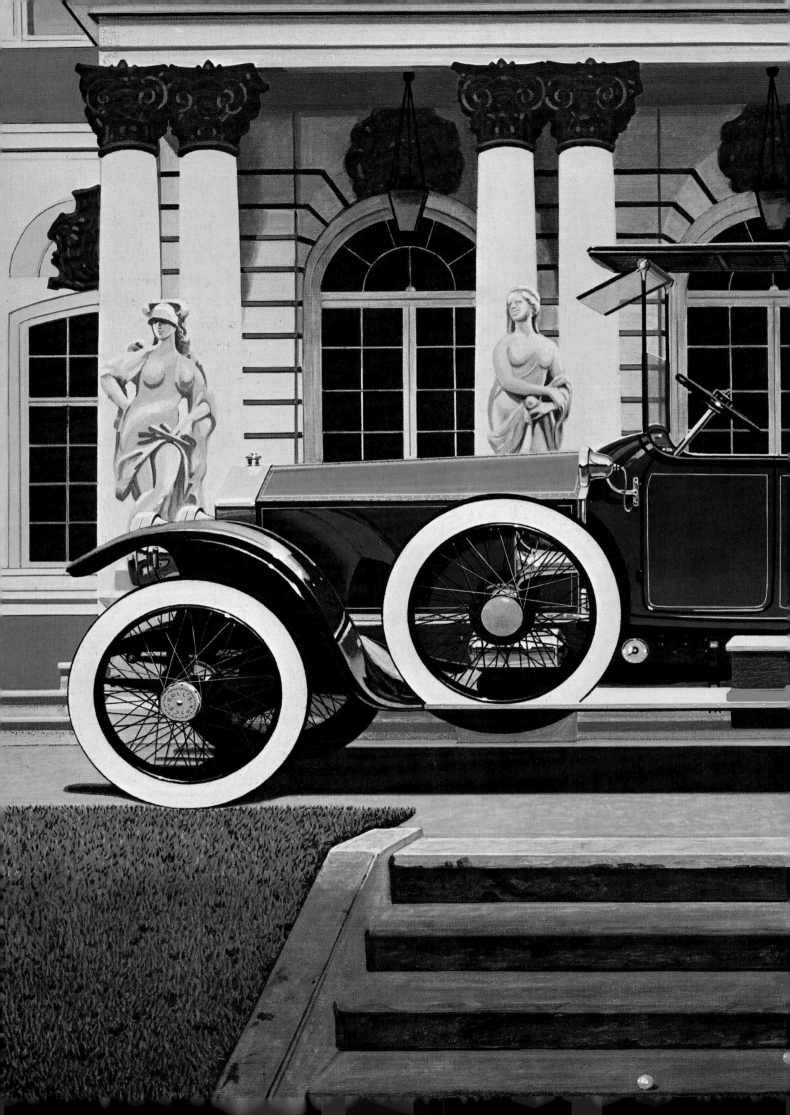

FIVE-SEATER TOURING CAR 1914

A year or so ago there was a television commercial which showed the humorous plight of two new automobile owners. Both people had been shopping and returned to the wrong cars. Understandable, since both cars were exactly alike. The confusion which ensued was very funny to watch, because the television viewer was not involved in the situation. But no doubt real situations of this sort do occur every day because the automobile manufacturers cannot offer a real "personalized" car to the millions of new car buyers every year.

This sort of thing can be very damaging to the ego of a man who has saved for a long time to buy the car of his dreams, only to discover some other man who had the same dream is right next to him at the first stoplight he reaches.

That didn't happen to Mr. and Mrs. Frederick Coleman, who, according to *The Autocar* of June 6, 1914, bought the Rolls-Royce Silver Ghost in this painting. The Colemans were able to go into the Rolls-Royce showroom and order precisely the kind of car they wanted, and they could be assured that it would be unlike any other.

The Colemans chose Cann, Ltd., to build the body for their car and asked for some unusual features. The car was to be finished in aluminum to show the beautiful design to good advantage. The body was to have only two doors—two wide doors that served both the front and rear compartments of the five-seater touring car. The upholstery was to be aluminum-colored leather, which would certainly complement the exterior finish of the car and cause comment. Even the wood paneling on the interior would retain the theme, being pickled sycamore of a shade to match aluminum.

Several other interesting design features were incorporated into this car. The side lamps were moved from their historic place on the scuttle to the front mudguards. There was almost a complete absence of trim or moldings. The front seats were of the armchair type and were adjustable.

Unusual design? Yes, but not really outlandish compared to some of the requests filled in the coachbuilding era of the motorcar. Some of the most challenging came from the fabled maharajahs of India. The Nizam of Hyderabad owned a whole stable of Rolls-Royce cars, and one of them had sterling silver trim on the entire car. Still other Indian princes had gold-encrusted bodies or thrones built on chassis.

Indian princes were not alone in wanting things a little different in their cars. At least one Rolls-Royce motorcar comes to mind which was built with a small (obviously) water closet in the rear compartment.

Perhaps the most humorous coachbuilding specialty is recalled in a story about a wealthy sheep rancher in Australia. The Rolls-Royce he ordered was to have the usual refinements, including a window behind the front seat which could be raised or lowered to separate the front seat from the rear. It seemed that the owner used to carry prize sheep in the rear compartment and they were inclined to lick his neck as he drove.

One of the most outstanding United States coachbuilders was Brewster and Company in New York. It was one of the prime body suppliers to the Rolls-Royce factory set up in Springfield, Massachusetts, in 1920. Contrary to the English practice, the American Rolls-Royce advertised complete vehicles, including bodies. In 1926, Brewster was bought by Rolls-Royce, and for the remaining five years that the Springfield plant operated, nearly all the output was bodied by Brewster.

The painter vividly recalls visiting Brewster's Long Island warehouse in 1938 and seeing floor after floor of used Rolls-Royce cars, almost any one of which could have been purchased for three or four hundred dollars.

You may wonder why the painter has placed a penny on edge on a Rolls-Royce radiator. This recalls a test which Claude Johnson made as yet another dramatic way of showing the lack of vibration in a Rolls-Royce motorcar. The engine was running when the penny was placed there. Try that on your car.

When the painter visited Stowe in England a few years ago, he was stopped by this 500-year-old arch. He realized it was of the same classic design that inspired the famous Rolls-Royce radiator. And so the setting for this Rolls-Royce was established in the painter's mind indelibly.

Until the 1940s, it was not hard for people like Mr. and Mrs. Coleman to find a custom coachbuilder and have a personal car built. Since World War II, however, the majority of the body-making firms have gone out of business. Italy still has several who produce many beautiful "one-off" and limited-production designs on exotic sports car chassis produced by Ferrari, Maserati, Lamborghini, and others. The great English firms of H. J. Mulliner and Park Ward were merged and absorbed by Rolls-Royce in 1961. The Studebaker Company, which began as carriage makers in South Bend, Indiana, and switched to motorcars in 1902, no longer exists as a car manufacturer. And all that is left of the American Fisher Body Company is a plaque on the doorplate of every General Motors car reading "Body by Fisher."

Melbourne Brindle

PRINCE YUSUPOV'S SIDE-LIGHT CABRIOLET 1914

A painter setting out to produce a book of paintings such as these has a tremendous advantage over a photographer attempting a similar work. The painter can create cars that no longer exist by using any photographs or other likenesses of the car.

This painting is a very good example of the story that a painter can tell on canvas with just a small given to start with. In this case, a single silhouetted black-and-white photograph from the files of a coachbuilder showed a side-light cabriolet and indicated that it was built for Prince Felix Yusupov. The rest was left up to the painter.

Through his long years of experience as an automotive enthusiast, the painter was able to select a color for Prince Yusupov's car that looked right. The real color was unknown. In addition, the painter knew the historic circumstances surrounding Prince Yusupov and was able to show this beautiful car in its historic perspective.

Rolls-Royce cars were popular in Russia during the years of Czar Nicholas II. The Czar owned two 1913 Silver Ghost landaulets, which were purchased by an English nobleman before Russia became the Union of Soviet Socialist Republics. The Czar's mother, Empress Marie, owned a Silver Ghost which is shown in this book.

That an English car should be so popular with Russian royalty is not so difficult to understand. King George V of England was related to just about every member of European, Russian, and Balkan royalty. The Czar of all the Russias was his cousin.

Empress Alexandra, Czarina of Russia, was a granddaughter of Queen Victoria who had been a female hemophilia carrier. Carriers do not suffer from the dreaded "bleeder's disease" but pass it on to their progeny. Thus it was that Alexandra was a carrier also, and her only son, Czarevich Alexis, heir to the Russian throne, was a hemophiliac.

The Empress knew she had brought the disease into the Romanov family. To ease her guilt for every pain Alexis suffered, she turned to prayer and spent hours each day praying for a miracle that would cure him.

The miracle came true, as far as she was concerned, when Gregory Rasputin, a peasant monk from Siberia, arrived in St. Petersburg in 1905. Rasputin claimed to have healing powers and had a large following among Russian court ladies who were much taken up with mysticism, rattling tables, and the like. The Empress, in her blind desire to help her son, became Rasputin's most ardent and influential follower. So great was her belief that by 1911 the monk was really the power behind the throne.

Most historians now believe that Rasputin was a hypnotist *extraordinaire*. He was a gigantic man, with long flowing hair and beard and eyes of the most incredible blue. These eyes gazed over the bodies of afflicted people while his voice intoned scripture. Soon those under his spell felt a soothing warmth and a sense of well-being that allayed their fears. Whether their afflictions were actually cured is in doubt, but they felt better about things after visiting the monk. The Czar, Czarina, and Czarevich were no exception.

96

Prince Felix Yusupov was an exception. Twenty-nine years old in 1916, he was heir to a fortune estimated at some five hundred million dollars, and married to the Czar's niece. He was a playboy at heart, and one of his toys was this Rolls-Royce. The car may have played an important part in the events during December of 1916 when Yusupov and his cohorts killed Rasputin.

Yusupov's fellow conspirators were Vladimir Purishkevich, a member of the Duma; Sukhotin, an army officer; Dr. Lazovert, an army physician; and Grand Duke Dimitry, a member of the royal family. The Prince knew that Rasputin was interested in his wife, Princess Irina, and, using her as bait, he got Rasputin to agree to a late evening visit to Yusupov's Moika Palace.

The date was set for December 29. Yusupov had a basement room prepared for Rasputin's visit. Dr. Lazovert ground cyanide of potassium crystals to powder and sprinkled it inside little cakes which Rasputin loved. A bottle of Madeira was also poisoned. In all, enough cyanide was used to kill dozens of men.

Near midnight, Yusupov drove to pick up Rasputin while the other conspirators lit several upstairs rooms in the palace and put loud march music records on the gramophone to indicate that a party was in progress. Rasputin remarked on all this gaiety when he and the Prince reached the palace. Yusupov said his wife was entertaining but that she would soon be down to see the monk.

Rasputin was led into the room and offered some of the cakes. According to Yusupov's account the monk ate two cakes, with no effect. These were followed by poisoned wine which still left Rasputin talking normally to his "little friend," as he called Yusupov. After two tense hours, a frightened Yusupov went upstairs to confer with his friends, who were visibly shaken. Lazovert had already fainted once from nerves. Yusupov took Dimitry's Browning pistol and returned to the room. He fired a shot into Rasputin's back and the monk slid to the floor.

Yusupov was joined by his friends. Dr. Lazovert felt the monk's pulse and pronounced him dead. The others left the room with the gun, and suddenly Rasputin came to life, yelling and grabbing for Yusupov. Scared out of his wits, the Prince shook free and ran upstairs yelling for Purishkevich to finish off the monk. Purishkevich followed a trail of blood out to the snowy courtyard where he found the dying man and fired several more shots. The others joined him in kicking and clubbing the body until it no longer moved. They then tied up the body and wrapped it in a curtain. They put the body in Yusupov's car and drove to the Neva River, where the body was dumped through a hole in the ice. It is this scene that the painter has captured.

A police investigation followed when Rasputin's boot was found near the hole, and three days later the body was recovered. Autopsy showed that Rasputin had finally died by drowning, after succeeding in getting his hands free. Poison, bullets, and water were required to kill the powerful Rasputin.

One thing remains a mystery. Rasputin had written a letter a few days before his death predicting that he would die before January 1, 1917. He told the Czar in the letter that if he were killed by royalists, then the Czar would not reign long, and his whole family would die with him.

Rasputin was killed by royalists before January 1, and the entire family of Nicholas II was killed in 1918, victims of the Russian Revolution.

"... I took the opportunity to pour the madeira into a glass containing cyanide ..."

Prince Felix Yusupov
La Fin de Rasputin 1919

Melbourne Brindle

CARROSSERIE SCHAPIRO-SCHEBERA SKIFF 1914

Automobile fanciers know that a variety of materials has been used for bodywork down through the years. Today, of course, steel bodies predominate on mass-produced cars. Plastic reinforced fiberglass is used on several low-production models. For very expensive cars of the "one-off" or small production type, aluminum is still preferred.

When motorcars first became popular after the turn of the century, most of the coachwork followed carriage body construction, being made mainly of wood, and steamed and warped to produce curved areas. A little later, in an effort to protect the wood from the elements, fabric was stretched across the wooden body parts and painted. This unique method was used on many types of cars right up to the 1930s.

By 1910, coachbuilders had begun to build body framework of strong wood, with sheet metal formed over the framework and nailed into the wood. This method of body construction has been used for years by many auto manufacturers, but today the only cars that come to mind with this kind of body are the British Morgan sports car and the Rolls-Royce Phantom V.

So we can see that, by 1914, wood was no longer a favorite external material for motorcar bodies. There were exceptions to that rule, naturally. Many enthusiasts will be familiar with the remarkable tulipwood Boulogne model built by Hispano-Suiza. That car, with its beautiful varnished wood planks, has been seen by thousands in books, magazines, and automobile shows. But after that beautiful car, what?

That was surely the way Dr. R. O. Barnard of Beckhams, Chiddingfold, Surrey, felt until a special day in 1955. It seemed that his friend and fellow Rolls-Royce enthusiast, Michael Vivian, had got word of a 1914 Silver Ghost with a boat body. Not boat-tailed, or boat-shaped, but wood-planked boat!

The car was in Egypt and was owned by a member of the Veteran Car Club. This owner, Vivian explained, had little use for the car and would lend it to any member who wanted to restore and look after it for awhile. After seeing photographs of the unusual car, Dr. Barnard and Mr. Vivian decided that they wanted to get their hands on the car no matter what the conditions.

When the car arrived on the quay in England, the two men approached it with a mixture of awe, admiration, and outright curiosity. The first task was to get it away from the docks, so they got at it. The engine wouldn't start at first, due to faulty electric equipment and a frozen clutch. Finally these problems were overcome and the engine ran for a short period. It didn't run long, since a fan blade had, at some point during its Egyptian labors, given up the ghost both figuratively and literally. It had flown out through the radiator.

Once the car was home, the two men tried to discover something about how it came into being, before starting the restoration. The skiff, as the body style was called, bore the number plate 54PB. Rolls-Royce records showed that cars with number plates 5PB to 65PB were D series cars from 1914. The chassis number was 45J. The car had the four-speed gearbox reintroduced in 1913. Rolls-Royce knew nothing about the car other than the fact that the chassis had left the Derby Works in 1914 to be delivered to the buyer in France. Now this unusual body . . .

The skiff bore the plate of Carrosserie Schapiro-Schebera of Berlin. At first nothing could be discovered about this German coachbuilding firm. It was not until years later that the men got in touch with Hans Neubauer, a German historian who was able to tell them something about the company.

Jacob Schapiro appeared in Berlin after World War I and bought the coachbuilding firm of Schebera. Mr. Neubauer felt that the body might have been designed by Ernst Neumann-Neander who produced boat-tailed designs for many German firms in the early 1920s. At the end of that decade, Mr. Schapiro had left Germany for the United States.

One can conclude, then, that chassis number 45J had a different body from 1914 to the 1920s, or that it remained a bare chassis during the war and was bodied after the armistice.

The restorers were pleased to find that the body had suffered little during its years of desert operation. Restoration became more of a boat-building problem than a coachwork problem. The construction was of the best "clinker-built" marine type. The wood had no rot, either wet or dry, although the top "deck" had been crushed a bit and needed rebuilding. After much sanding and varnishing, everything was in good order. All the trim was re-nickeled, and the upholstery was redone in green hide, deep-buttoned in a diamond pattern.

Now it was time for the mechanical restoration, and here Dr. Barnard and Mr. Vivian were in for a pleasant surprise. Dismantling the engine proved that the car had done few miles. All it required was new piston rings on the original cast-iron pistons.

The car's history since 1914 was full of rumors. During the restoration, Barnard and Vivian found a card under one of the seats bearing the name "Nagred Bay, Canoe," and felt certain this had been the original owner of the skiff Ghost.

At some point in its life, the car was in the possession of Mohammed Ali, brother of King Fuad. It was in the royal stables until Mohammed's nephew, King Farouk, got rid of it as part payment for some debt.

A British officer stationed in Egypt later salvaged the car from a lot and used it until he died suddenly in the 1951 riots. From him, the car passed to the Veteran Car Club member. When this gentleman arrived in England during the car's restoration by Barnard and Vivian, he consented to sell it to them.

It is a dramatic contrast from the sands of Egypt, upon which the painter has placed the car, to the Surrey garden aglow with the vivid colors of Dr. Barnard's superb collection of heather. It was this garden that inspired the vignette at the lower left. In the larger view, we see this interesting Silver Ghost in the setting where it seemingly spent most of its career. In the other we see it now retired to a pleasant life in the English countryside.

The dagger, used by the painter to write the car's plate number in the sand, came from the tomb of King Tutankhamen. The scabbard which held the blade for six centuries waits nearby.

Melbourne Brindle

ROLLS-ROYCE
ARMORED CAR 1914

It's easy to look at these automobiles of sixty years ago and admire them for their beauty and value alone. But the admiration should not stop there, for these cars had reliability and toughness engineered-in to a degree that cannot be matched today.

Just take a modern luxury sedan and strip it down to the bare chassis. Add about 4½ tons of armor plating, then drive it to the nearest desert and run it around on the dunes for weeks on end at top speed. Perhaps you don't think it can be done? Rolls-Royce did it to many Silver Ghost chassis during World War I, and, in the hands of men like Colonel T. E. Lawrence, these cars gained the respect of friends and were feared by foes.

The first Rolls-Royce armored cars were built for the Royal Navy, amazingly enough. These ships of land formed the design pattern which became standard. The radiator, bonnet, and driving compartment were shielded completely by $^3/_8$-inch armor plate. Immediately behind the driver was a steel-encased turret 5 feet wide. The turret moved a full 360 degrees, giving the machine gunner a complete field of fire in any direction.

The only major changes to the stock chassis involved fitting thirteen-leaf springs in front, fifteen-leaf springs in the rear to support the tons of extra weight. Later, double rear tires were added to improve traction on sand.

Under fire, the hinged doors in front of the radiator could be closed. It is hard to imagine an engine sturdy enough to pull several tons of metal and a crew of two or three men at top speed through hot desert sands with little or no air passing through the radiator. But this was common practice and the cars suffered no ill effects other than letting off steam every so often.

Early in 1915, the first squadrons of armored cars were ready for action. By this time, the war in Europe had settled down to dreary trench combat and the speedy land cruisers were hard put to find running room to aid the war effort. They were soon to find their rightful place in the scheme of things.

The Duke of Westminster took his unit to German West Africa to aid General Botha in his campaign there. The cars were especially effective against German cavalry. They would lie hidden until the enemy horsemen came near; then the bright head-lights would snap on and the machine guns would go to work on the stampeding horses and riders. After four months of such grueling operations through endless brush, dry river beds, and tropical heat, the only mechanical difficulties involved a bent steering rod and a broken oil pump.

The Duke and his cars were later transferred to Egypt, where the Rolls-Royce armored car truly came into its element. After nine months of heroic work, the crews finally gave out due to heat and casualty attrition, and the cars were sent home to England for a well-deserved rest.

Inevitably, the prowess of the Rolls-Royce armored car came to the attention of the legendary Lawrence of Arabia, Colonel T. E. Lawrence. Lawrence was a desert fighter without peer and he was quick to realize the advantages these new weapons would give him in his battle against the Turks in Arabia.

Under his command, the heavily laden cars would cruise the desert at speeds up to 70 miles per hour, bringing death and destruction to the enemy. Lawrence liked to call this kind of Rolls-Royce warfare, "fighting deluxe."

His fleet of nine armored cars and two Rolls-Royce tenders gave his command amazing mobility. One of his drivers, S. C. Rolls (no relation to C. S. Rolls), gives us a sample of this mobility in his book, *Steel Chariots in the Desert*. ". . . Lawrence took three of them and captured two Turkish posts, blew up a bridge, wiped out a Kurdish cavalry regiment, blew up another bridge, and ripped up six hundred pairs of rails— thereby throwing the whole Turkish supply system into chaos—all in one day!" Rolls, incidentally, often finished a day's driving with bruised and bleeding hands after constant zig-zagging to avoid obstacles, and equally constant gear changing to keep his Ghost moving through soft sand.

Lawrence and his men lived dangerously as they improvised a new kind of desert warfare. One of the near-misses from death took place while Lawrence played his favorite sport, train wrecking. Working from a Rolls-Royce tender with Rolls at the wheel, Lawrence went to set the charge. When the next train came along, he lit the fuse and ran for the car. The engine of the train disappeared in a cloud of steam when the thunderous explosion ripped it from the tracks. Fractions of a second later, Rolls felt a heavy thump on the seat next to him. A large section of twisted rail had missed him by inches, and missed Lawrence by a few seconds. Had he been faster on his feet, Lawrence would surely have been crushed by the rail.

The tales go on and on. They are to be found in every work about Colonel Lawrence. Lawrence himself said, "A Rolls in the desert was above rubies. . . ."

After the Armistice, Lawrence had an interview with Lowell Thomas, who has passed the comments on to us in his book *With Lawrence in Arabia*. At the interview's end, Thomas asked what Lawrence would most like to have. Lawrence summed up his admiration for Rolls-Royce motorcars: "I should like to have a Rolls-Royce car with enough tires and petrol to last me all my life."

The car in the painting is identical to those sent to Lawrence's Hedjaz Armored Car Unit at Siwa Oasis, Arabia, in 1917. Amid the wreckage caused by Lawrence's "sport" is a dynamite brick of the type used by him in 1917. An Anzac medal commemorates the landing of Anzac forces at Gallipoli in 1915.

The painted "photograph" at left shows Lawrence in his desert garb of kaffiyeh and agal. The other photo shows him astride the motorcycle on which he was later killed near his Dorset home on May 13, 1935.

"A Rolls in the desert is worth more than rubies"
T. E. Lawrence... *Seven Pillars of Wisdom*

PALMER CORD TYRE

Melbourne Brindle

ON THE FOLLOWING PAGES ARE...

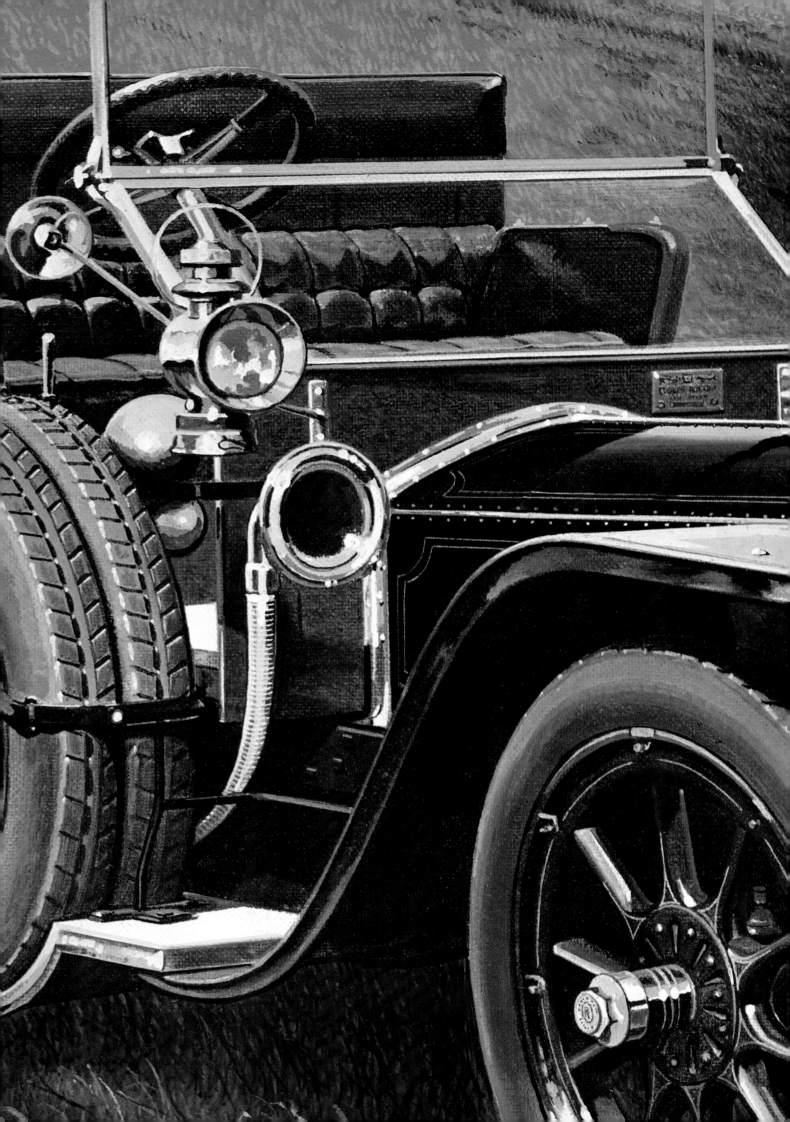

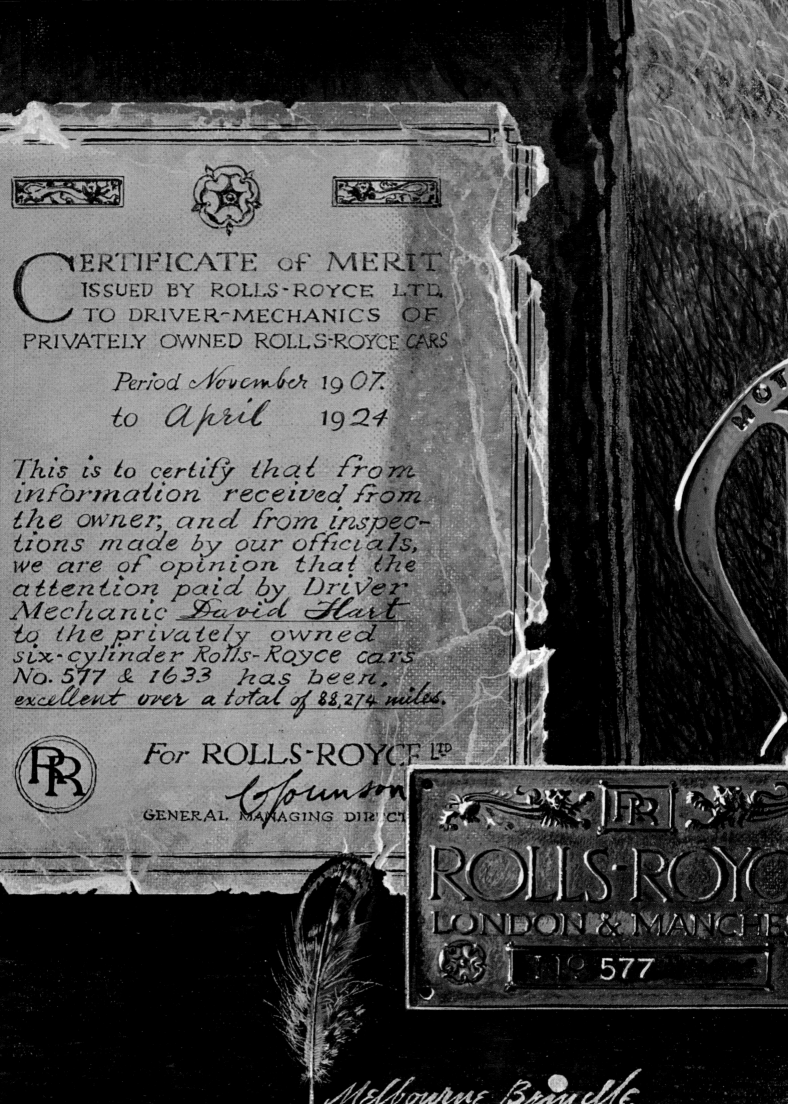

CERTIFICATE of MERIT
ISSUED BY ROLLS-ROYCE LTD.
TO DRIVER-MECHANICS OF
PRIVATELY OWNED ROLLS-ROYCE CARS

Period *November* 19 07.
to *April* 1924

This is to certify that from information received from the owner, and from inspections made by our officials, we are of opinion that the attention paid by Driver Mechanic *David Hart* to the privately owned six-cylinder Rolls-Royce cars No. 577 & 1633 has been excellent over a total of 88,274 miles.

For ROLLS-ROYCE LTD

Johnson
GENERAL MANAGING DIRECTOR

ROLLS-ROYC
LONDON & MANCHE
1 19 577

IN THIS ROLLS-ROYCE SILVER GHOST, HIS
& THE PRINCE OF WALES, VISITED EUROP

PARIS { LIVERPOOL
MANCHESTER
CHESTER & PRESTON

DISTINCTIVE COMPONENTS OF A SILVER GHOST

First - The Name

Rolls-Royce - the name rolls as smoothly over the tongue as the car does over the road. There have been other hyphenated names that stood for fine cars. Hispano-Suiza, Stevens-Duryea, Pierce-Arrow, De Dion-Bouton, Isotta-Fraschini, and others. But none, however grand it may be in the eyes of some, conjures up the image that the world associates with Rolls-Royce. Our vocabulary is richer for the magic in that name. We see the proud clean-cut radiator - bearing the entwined initials and surmounted by the Charles Sykes masterpiece. Just saying Rolls-Royce is a celebration of excellence.

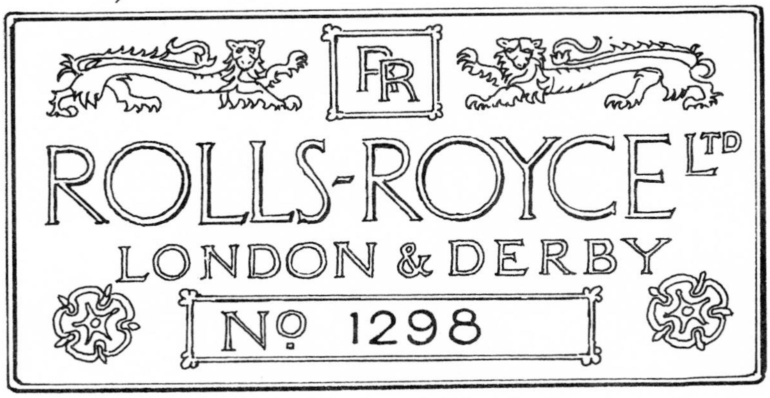

The Plaque

Any research on a Rolls-Royce must begin here. for the plaque gives the chassis

number and the works designation for each car. Cast of nickel silver or brass, it is heavy in the hand. The design is worthy of a master jeweller to the crown. On early Silver Ghosts it may be found on the bulkhead where the long

120

bonnet terminates. Later on it was hidden under the bonnet. During the history of Rolls-Royce there have been three different addresses on the plaques. London and Manchester until 1908, London and Derby until 1939, and London and Crewe to the present.

Ignition and Throttle Controls. Sit behind the wheel of a Silver Ghost and right in front of you, in the center of the steering wheel is the quadrant for the spark and throttle controls. The design of this element is different from that of any other car in appearance and performance. Take hold of the spark lever

on the right. The round black knob feels just right in the fingers. Push down lightly, it is spring-loaded and will move effortlessly to "early" or "late" – not "advance" and "retard" as on ordinary cars. The throttle lever, on the left duplicates the feel and moves to "fast" or "slow" instead of "open" or "shut." After 1911, the ignition switch and fuel-mixture control were moved from the dashboard to a combined control in the center of the quadrant. At the top is a delicately tapered lever which enables the driver to control his fuel mixture from "weak" to "strong". Below that is a raised knurled knob which controls the ignition function. It has four positions, B for battery ignition; M for magneto ignition; M and B for simultaneous magneto and battery ignition; and O which shuts the engine off.

The <u>Steering Wheel</u>. A driver gets the feel of the car through his hands on the steering wheel, so the design of the wheel is very important. The indentations on the underside of a Silver Ghost steering wheel are deep and spaced just right to receive the fingers. Lozier and Mercer were two other manufacturers who invented steering wheels in a similar fashion, but not in just the proper way Rolls-Royce did. The smooth black wheel material extends well down the sculptured aluminum spokes, so that the hand feels comfortable anywhere down

on the wheel. Halfway the slender steering column is an enclosure housing a bearing with a small oil cup attached. Still further down on the steering column of touring cars is another typical Rolls-Royce touch— a steeply mounted tubular brace to strengthen the steering column. On enclosed cars, the steering column is shorter and is bolted to the bulkhead for support. It was also available in a choice of rakes, from A to D. At the base of the steering column is the steering box of cast aluminum with the Rolls-Royce emblem in bold relief. Steering linkage to the front wheels is by adjustable ball-and-socket design. The entire Silver Ghost steering assembly is an extremely efficient example of beauty, good design, and superlative engineering.

The Rolls-Royce Radiator. First shown to the world on the 1904 Rolls-Royce cars, the design has proved so simple and chaste that it has come down to us on the present Rolls-Royce cars. This radiator, as seen on an approaching Silver Ghost presents the distinctive image known so well throughout the world. The radiator on all Silver Ghosts is mounted directly above the axle.

The Front Axle. Very early Silver Ghosts used an I-beam front axle with a deeply dropped center section. The design of this multi-curved front axle was at odds with the clean angular lines of the radiator above it. By 1909, the curve in the center section had become somewhat shallower. Then someone in the Rolls-Royce operation with a designer's eye created the perfect Silver Ghost front axle. It first appeared in August of 1909, and remained unchanged until 1925.

It is the perfect complement to the famous radiator. Notice how the end sections closely repeat the radiator's angle. The small Vickers nickel steel stamping in the center of the axle also repeats the angles of the radiator. The king pins are set at just the right angle so that, combined with the wheel camber, they meet

precisely
at the center of
the tire as it contacts the road. The result is
effortless steering control. Altogether the axle
is a perfect example of good design emanating
from attention to detail.

The Artillery-Type Wheels. Of all the vast number
of wooden artillery-type wheels designed for
motorcars between 1907 and 1925, those of Rolls-
Royce were in a class by themselves from a
designer's point of view. One fine American car

comes close—the Locomobile. During this period, when tires stood high and were thin in section, wooden wheels tended to look spidery. Not those of Rolls-Royce. Silver Ghost wheels look powerful and rugged, which indeed they are. Early Ghosts had nondetachable rims, while later models featured the Wayland Dual Rim which attached to the wheel with eight bolts. Only on a Rolls-Royce will you find ten-spoked front wheels, and fourteen spoked rear wheels. Since the power was applied at the rear wheels, they are as strong as they look. The front wheels controlled the car, but did not need the added spokes for strength. The cutout design of the felloes is pure Rolls-Royce. The crowning touch to these wheels is the beautifully designed hupcap.

The Hubcaps. Hubcaps on a Silver Ghost are in just the right proportion to the wheel, especially on the artillery-type rear wheels. These important parts also help a viewer to identify the car from either side as a Rolls-Royce. Motorcars such as Rolls-Royce, with full-floating rear axles, had a definate advantage over other types because the hubcaps had to be large enough to encompass the hub at the end of the driving axles. The hubcaps on the front wheels are smaller.

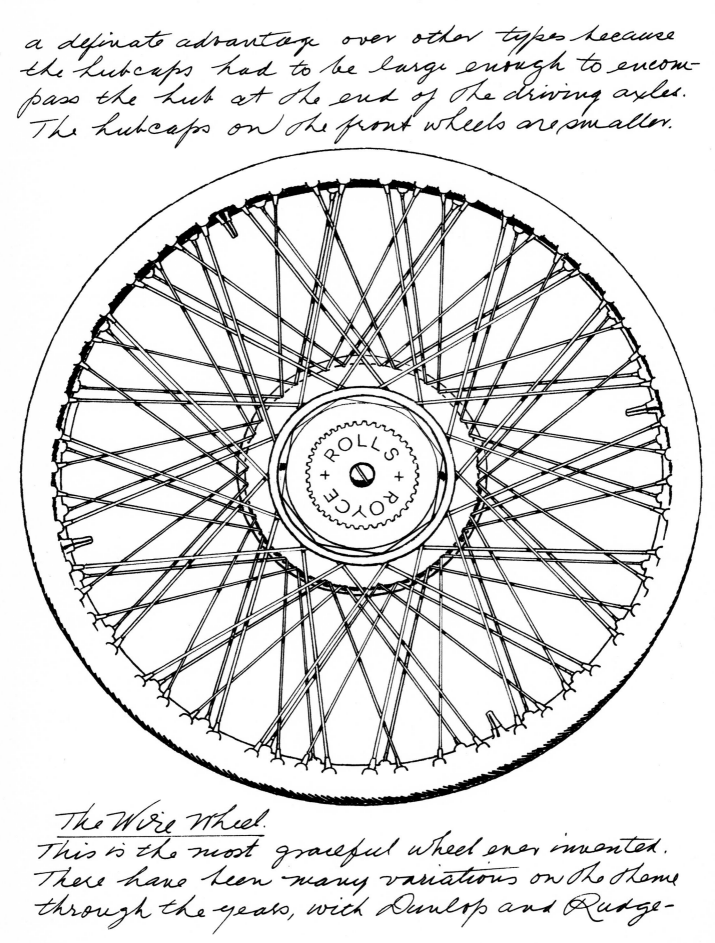

The Wire Wheel.
This is the most graceful wheel ever invented. There have been many variations on the theme through the years, with Dunlop and Rudge-

Whitworth the best examples. Aesthetically there is not too much difference between them, but from an engineering standpoint the Dunlop is perhaps superior. The locking principle on the Dunlop wheel is excellent. The wheel is locked securely to the hub by a series of serrations and by a spring-loaded inner hubcap in the hub itself, with a free-turning outer serrated ring. This outer ring is attached to the hub shell. To mount the wheel on the hub, the inner serrated hubcap is depressed by a special wrench which tightens the outer ring to the hub. The inner serrated portion is then released to mate with the outer serrations, providing a positive lock which prevents the wheel from becoming loose on the road. Watch a well-enameled wire wheel on a Rolls-Royce under way and note how each spoke catches the sunlight! The

wire spokes
above the hub
suspend the
weight of the car. (On a wooden wheel the
spokes below the hub support the weight)
Another characteristic of a Silver Ghost
wire wheel is its extra long tapered hub.
The length of the hub dictates the accute
angle of the spokes. Seen from the front,
this angle seems to repeat the angle
of the radiator and the front axle.
The combination looks just right on
a Rolls-Royce.

The Gear and Brake Levers.

These delicate-appearing levers are sturdy without seeming to be so, because they carry no excess weight. They make gear changing and braking a pleasure on a Rolls-Royce Silver Ghost. When shifting gears a feather touch is all that is needed, since the gears respond smoothly. The nickel close-plated levers emerge from their quadrant on the outside of the frame rail. (Close-plating consists of soldering a sheet of nickel about .006 inch thick onto the parts. Rolls-Royce did not nickel-plate by electrolysis, which is the less expensive method) If the car was trimmed in brass, the levers were "brassed-over" to match. They were often exposed to view outside the body. All London-Edinburgh models had exposed levers for the sporting look and these seemingly intricate controls added to the interest to be found in plain sight on many other Rolls-Royce models.

131

The Trussed Frame. This combination of angular (later tubular) cross members, tapering side rails, and two trusses — one under each side rail — could stand unbelievable punishment. The cross members strengthen the frame laterally, and the trusses strengthen vertically. During World Wars I and II, three to four tons of armor plate, plus crew and equipment were carried on the standard chassis, making up the famous Rolls-Royce armored car. Not one frame sagged, broke, or bent under the strain during arduous service. When the wars were over, many armored cars were returned to England and had passenger car coachwork installed. This is perhaps the best demonstration of the Rolls-Royce concept that the frame is the foundation of a well-built motorcar. Perhaps Mr. Royce had noticed the trusses fitted underneath railway carriages and fully appreciated their load-bearing qualities

The Square-Headed Bolt. As typically Rolls-Royce as the radiator, square-headed bolts are found throughout the car, principally for holding frame components

together. Only Rolls-Royce used this type of bolt. Other makers used rivets. Before valances came into vogue to cover the naked- ness of the chassis side members, the tidy appear- ance of many square bolt heads lined up along the frame lent a distinctive touch to a Silver Ghost. The last quarter of the bolt - just behind the square head - is tapered to fit a reamed hole. The bolt was fitted snugly up to the taper and driven home under pressure to insure a perfect fit. Mr Royce believed that a tapered bolt, carefully fitted, would hold frame components together better than a rivet. Examination of the frames of Silver Ghosts bears this out. Square headed bolts also made a chassis easier to repair should something go awry. With use of the correct wrench, the square head of the bolt never became round through maltreatment.

<u>The</u> <u>Carburetor</u>. This is one of the most sensitive pieces of equipment on the early motorcar engines. Some were wonderful to look at, all shining brass, knurled knobs and the like— but generally of questionable performance. Others were downright ugly. The Rolls-Royce Silver Ghost carburetor was a beauty in looks and operation. During a trip to England to gather information for this book, the painter rode many miles in Mr S. J. Skinner's 1910 Silver Ghost. He was impressed with the way the car started when cold — and it always started immediately when hot. The carburetor on Mr Skinner's car is the one illustrated here. One of the many pleasures of owning a Silver Ghost certainly must be that breathless moment when the bonnet is raised and the full impact of the famous 40/50 horsepower six cylinder engine is felt. Brass and copper and more brass

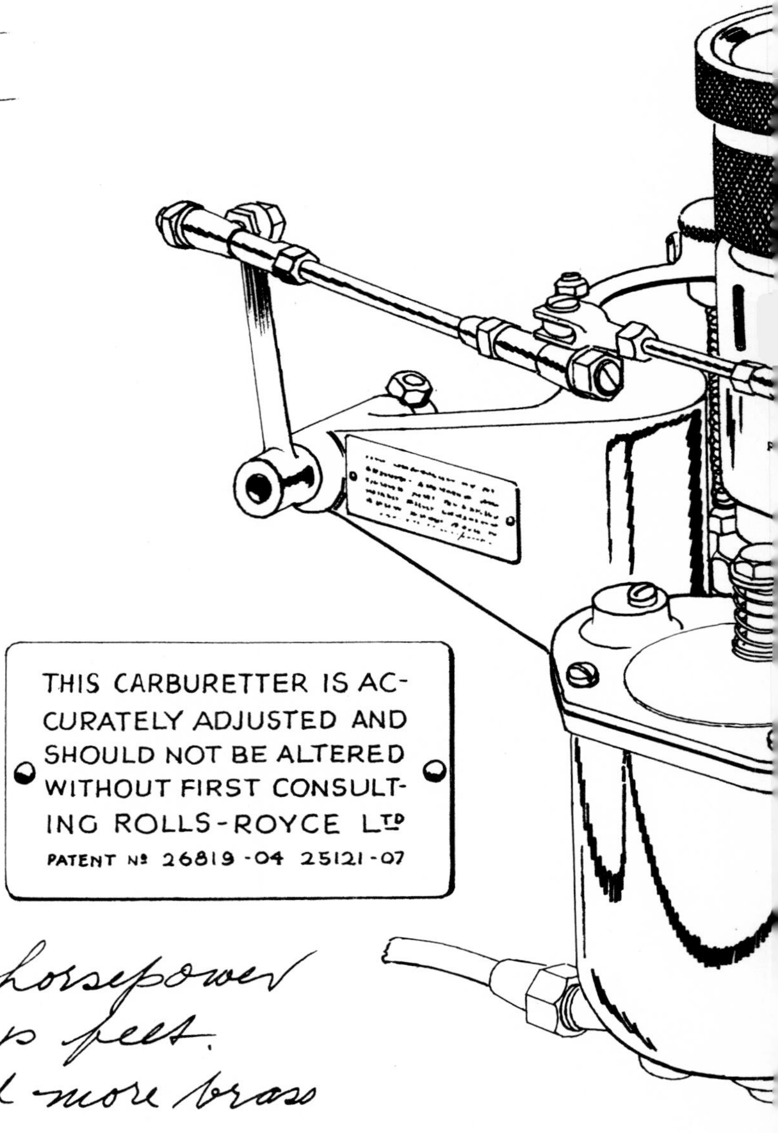

THIS CARBURETTER IS AC-CURATELY ADJUSTED AND SHOULD NOT BE ALTERED WITHOUT FIRST CONSULT-ING ROLLS-ROYCE L™

PATENT N° 26819-04 25121-07

and copper – and the most exciting piece of equipment is the carburetor. No excess metal on this item! Each piece of it is pared, shaped, and arranged just so. The ball-and-socket joints on the control linkage show to good advantage in the sketch. Contrary to the legend, Rolls-Royce did not seal the carburetor at the factory. The company did attach a plate with the legend shown here. The carburetor on the painter's Phantom I Rolls-Royce had knurled brass turnings on the tops which were almost identical to those on the carburetor shown here which were produced nineteen years earlier.

The Cantilever Spring. This type of rear spring first appeared on a Silver Ghost in 1911. The 1907 Silver Ghost had platform springing. Ghosts for the next three years had three quarter elliptic rear springs. A photograph of the first London-Edinburgh of 1911 shows cantilever springs set at an angle because the spring hangers were below the rear axle. Later models show flat cantilevers, with the rear spring tips sliding in trunnions above the axle. The number of leaves in the springs depended upon the body weight which would rest on the chassis. The long thin leaves were built up to accommodate the weight and still provide the flexibility for a comfortable ride. The eyes of the springs are forged solid, not wrapped. Rolls-Royce adopted this proceedure in testing done with a "bumping machine" built to simulate continental touring prior to the 1913 Alpine Trials. Long after other auto

makers had covered frames and springs with metal valances, as though ashamed of frames and springs, Rolls-Royce proudly displayed those long comfortable cantilever springs.

<u>The Trembler Coil.</u>   Henry Royce was a master electrician, so he was bound to create a distinctive and unusual coil box. Up to late 1912, the box was found mounted on the polished aluminum bulkhead on the passenger's side of the front compartment. After the tapered bonnets came into style, it was mounted on the bulkhead under the bonnet. The box looks rich and handsome, with the lower half of polished oak, skillfully dovetailed, and the upper half polished aluminum with the familiar Rolls-Royce rivets. Centered on top of the removable upper half is another chassis number plaque. Tacked inside the lid is a printed set of instructions for the proper maintenance of the coils. What could be a more logical place?

INSTRUCTIONS FOR ROLLS-ROYCE COILS

Do not in any way upset the adjustment of the tremblers until you are <u>sure</u> they require it.

Should the platinum points require truing up, they should be made <u>quite flat</u> with a <u>dead smooth</u> file.

The iron armature spring blade should not be altered in any way.

The spring blade carrying the platinum point is curved slightly upwards to ensure slight pressure on platinum pointed screw when this is adjusted.

To adjust the platinum point start with the points quite apart, turn on the battery current, screw down the screw (with the check screw partly tightened) slowly until the action of the trembler shows the points have just come into contact, then give the screw a further ¼ of a turn, which will ensure good contact and the correct amount of play for the iron armature, viz. 1/100 of an inch.

For reference please quote <u>L069</u>

137

The Fuel Tank. In motoring's early days, the passengers in the front seat sat above the fuel tank, which was tucked away under the cushions. Rolls-Royce was one of the first to change that, since it was inconvenient for the front passengers to alight from the car every time fuel was needed. The very first tank to appear on the rear of a Rolls-Royce was the perfect shape for a fuel tank—oval—and retained the shape until the last Silver Ghost was made. The designers of the tank used rivets lavishly in keeping with the style of the bonnet. The tank was insulated from the car by the use of bronze cups, which were incorporated into the mounts at either end. Two brackets for tail lamps were provided on each side of the tank, although only one tail lamp was used. The other bracket was used when touring on the continent, where other rules of the road applied and the tail lamp was moved over.

The Reserve Oil Tank. The painter can recall no other car in the world that mounted a reserve oil tank in the Rolls-Royce manner. It is located on the frame siderail, on the near side of the car in a place of equal importance with the side lamp, which is found just above and slightly behind it. It was designed to be functional as well as decorative, being finished in either nickel silver, or in brass. Remember, these cars were driven before the days when filling stations were plentiful, and so it must have been a comfort to know that the oil tank was filled with fresh oil, ready if needed.

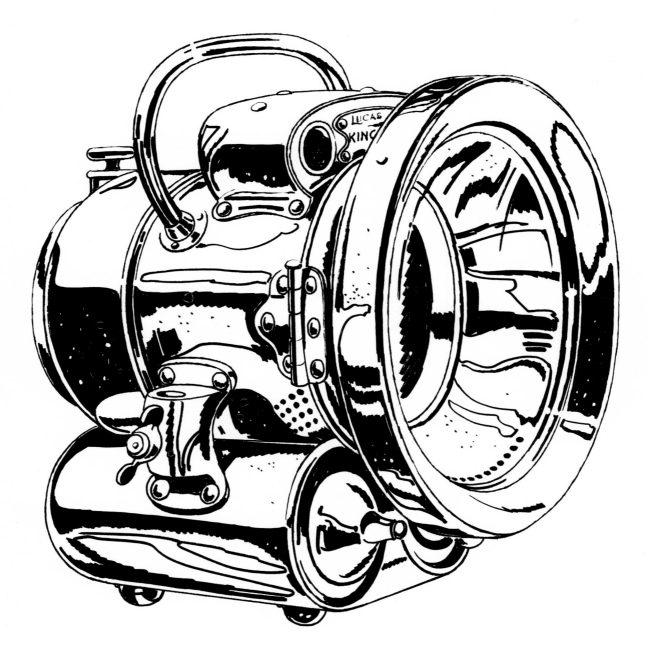

The Self-Generating Head Lamps. Rolls-
Royce never made their own lighting equipment.
The purchaser of a Silver Ghost chassis consult-
ing with the coachbuilder of his choice, was free
to select the lighting equipment he fancied.
Having viewed many early Silver Ghosts, the
painter believes that the majority chose Lucas
lighting. On reviewing his on-the-spot sketches

of several, however, he finds that the head lamps of the Maharajah of Mysore's car, Number 1683, are built by "Powell and Hanmer Ltd, manufactured in Birmingham". The boat-tailed skiff 54 P.B. is equipped with lamps made by "C. A. Vandervell & Co., London". Those on the Tulip-back limousine are made in America by "Rushmore Dynamo Works, Plainfield, New Jersey. Rushmore Lamps Limited, Distributors, 16 Brewer Street, Piccadilly Circus. London". (The Rushmore lamps are not self-generating. The gas for them is made in a separate generator tank on the running board. Rushmore called it "The Automatic Shaking Grate Generator".) The lamps illustrated here are by Lucas and are about the most beautiful the painter has seen. They are good examples of the self generating type. Water is held in the cylindrical container that makes up the body of the lamp. Two tanks below contain carbide (One is a spare and is brought into use by means of a (lever) The water drips on the carbide, man-ufacturing the gas for the lamps. The lamps can be removed easily for cleaning and storage by using the graceful carrying handle, and are replaced and secured by hand tightened wing-nuts. Each lamp carries a small plaque reading "Lucas-King of the Road".

The Tail Lamp. After the introduction of the oval fuel tank, a single tail lamp was in evidence on the rear of every Rolls-Royce Silver Ghost. The one illustrated here is from Mr Skinner's car. However, as a tribute to the oldest Ghost of them all, the 1907 company car, the painter has taken the liberty of show-ing the famous 1907 license plate-number A-X-201-behind the tail lamp. What more fitting way to end This section of the book than with this final tribute to the Silver Ghost, the model that earned the title "The Best Car in the World"

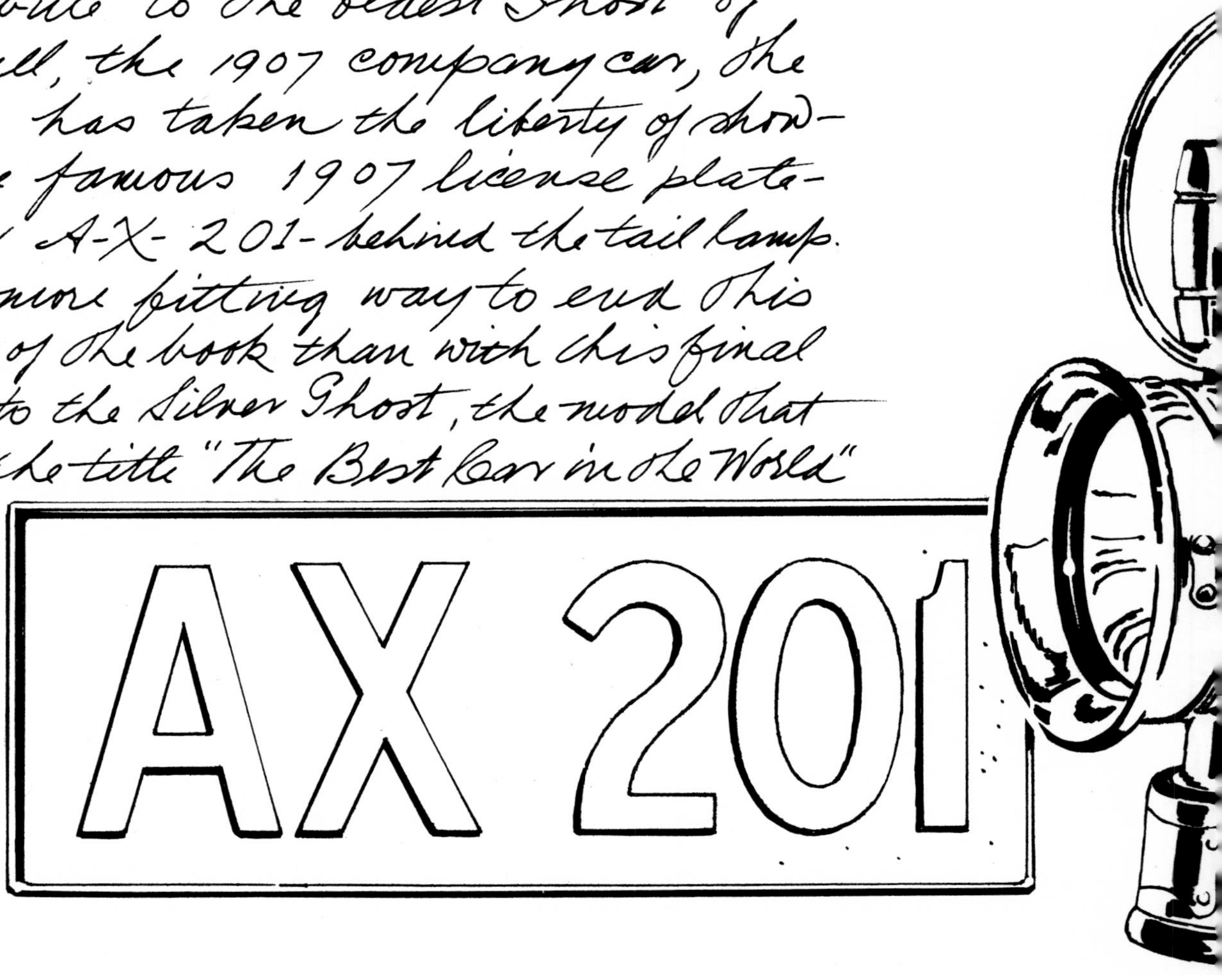

Postscript. This last gem, the wooden "valve holder" just about sums up the way the painter feels about Rolls-Royce's constant attention to detail. Nothing was too much bother. The way in which the valve head is recessed into the wooden case insures that the valve seat can not be damaged, either in transit, or while lying in a toolbox. The valve is in its oaken case, just as it left the factory so many years ago. It was shown to the painter almost as an after-thought by Mr Skinner while talking "shop" in his motorshed. The painter's sketchbook was just about full with notes and sketches, but he had to have this one! It was the last sketch in the sketchbook, and it's the last in this section

M.B.

143

MR. MULLINER'S LETTER...

Bayworth
63 Terminus Avenue
Bexhill
Sussex.

Dear Mr. Melburn Brindle Esq.

I have just received a letter from
G. McGregor Gray, enclosing me a copy of a
letter he has received from you, in which
you ask for various particulars, as to colour
etc of the Rolls Royce I built for Rolls,

As I retired from my Business in 1910, it is
difficult to remember the correct answers to
your questions

I am therefore sending your letter to Mr
Watts, asking them, if possible, to let me
have the information, but it may be some
time before I can write you again

I am sending you under separate cover
& by overland route some photos of old cars
which may perhaps interest you

Your sincerely Hy Mulliner
H.J. MULLINER

THE HON. C. S. ROLLS AND MR. H.

ROLLS & MULLINER on early Rolls
Bodywork & Bonnet painted a
Crimson, upper panels & Back
& simply varnished
Wings & Wheels Black, all plated
with Side Lamps and Wind screen
in nickel. Canvas Hood with
wooden slats

ON-THE-SPOT JOTTINGS
OF DETAILS NOTED IN THE FIELD

*Made on odd bits of near-at-hand paper, they indicate the need
for minute observation of detail . . . facts and general Rolls-
Royciana needed to execute the paintings. How many rivets in the
length of a Silver Ghost bonnet? How many leaves in a front spring . . .
a rear? What is the length of the steering column . . . and its
relation to the gear shift levers? Count those serrations in the hub
of a Dunlop wire wheel. The famous radiator of a Silver Ghost has
been referred to as square. Well, is it? So it was carefully
measured, with interesting results. It isn't square at all . . . it
just looks square. Noted too, the fact that the angle of the filler
cap on a Silver Ghost radiator closely repeats the angle of the radiator
below it. So it went, car after car, even to the carefully copied
signature of Stenson Cooke, secretary of the Royal Automobile Club
of 1909.*

.INER ON A NEW SIX-CYLINDER ROLLS-ROYCE.

B 47721

1906
RICH

straighten
up lamps.

Is body painted aluminum?
It is not made of aluminum
and left natural metal?

colors?
Royal vengue..

Patent leather
mudguard..?

R.C. 230

PALMER
CORD TYRE

These tyres look like
semi balloon —
check the maker.

Upholstery?
color?

Silver Ghost

Running board color
and covering.

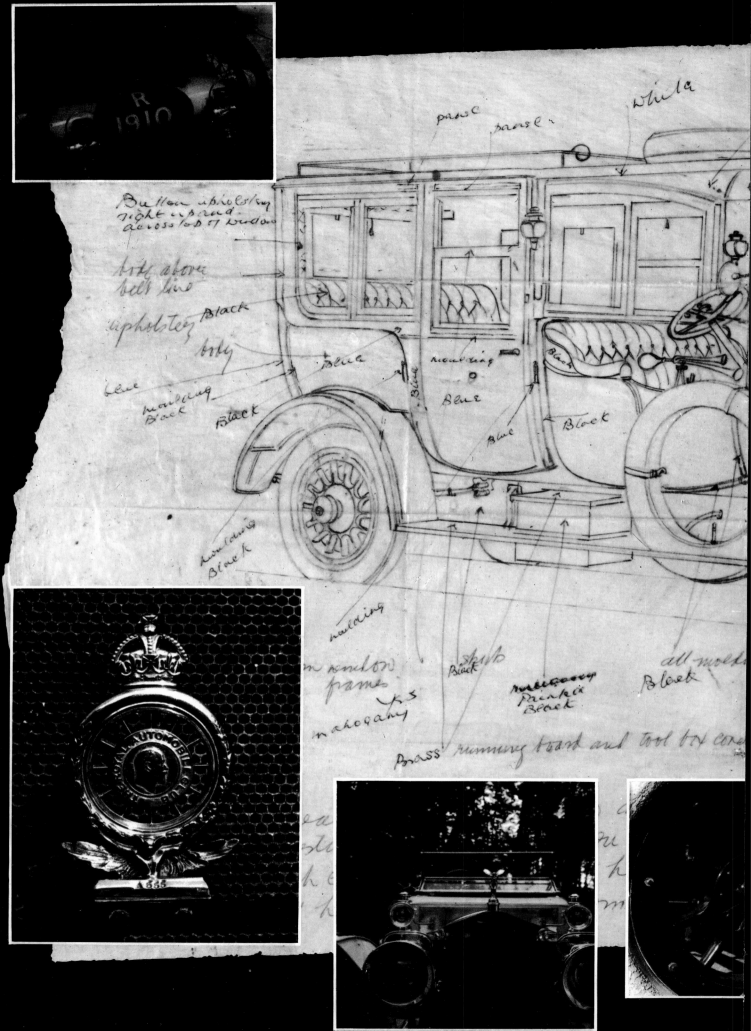

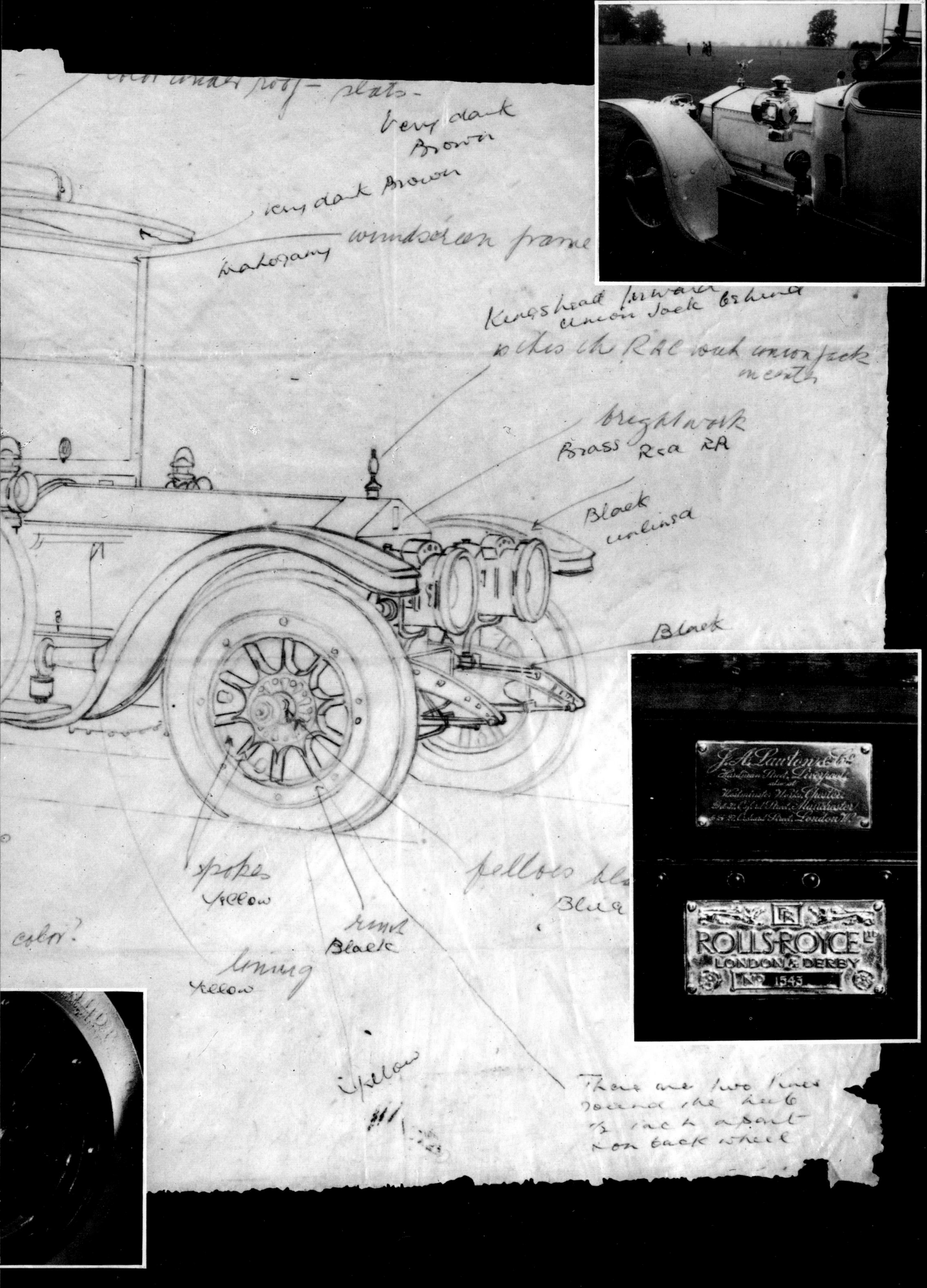

roll unclu roof - slats -
very dark
Brown

very dark Brown

Mahogany windscreen frame

Kingshead forward
union Jack behind
is this the RAC with union jack
wreath

brightwork
Brass Rca RR

Black
unlined

Black

color?

spokes
yellow

rim
Black

lining
Yellow

felloes black
Blue

Yellow

There are two lines
round the hub
½ inch apart
on back wheel

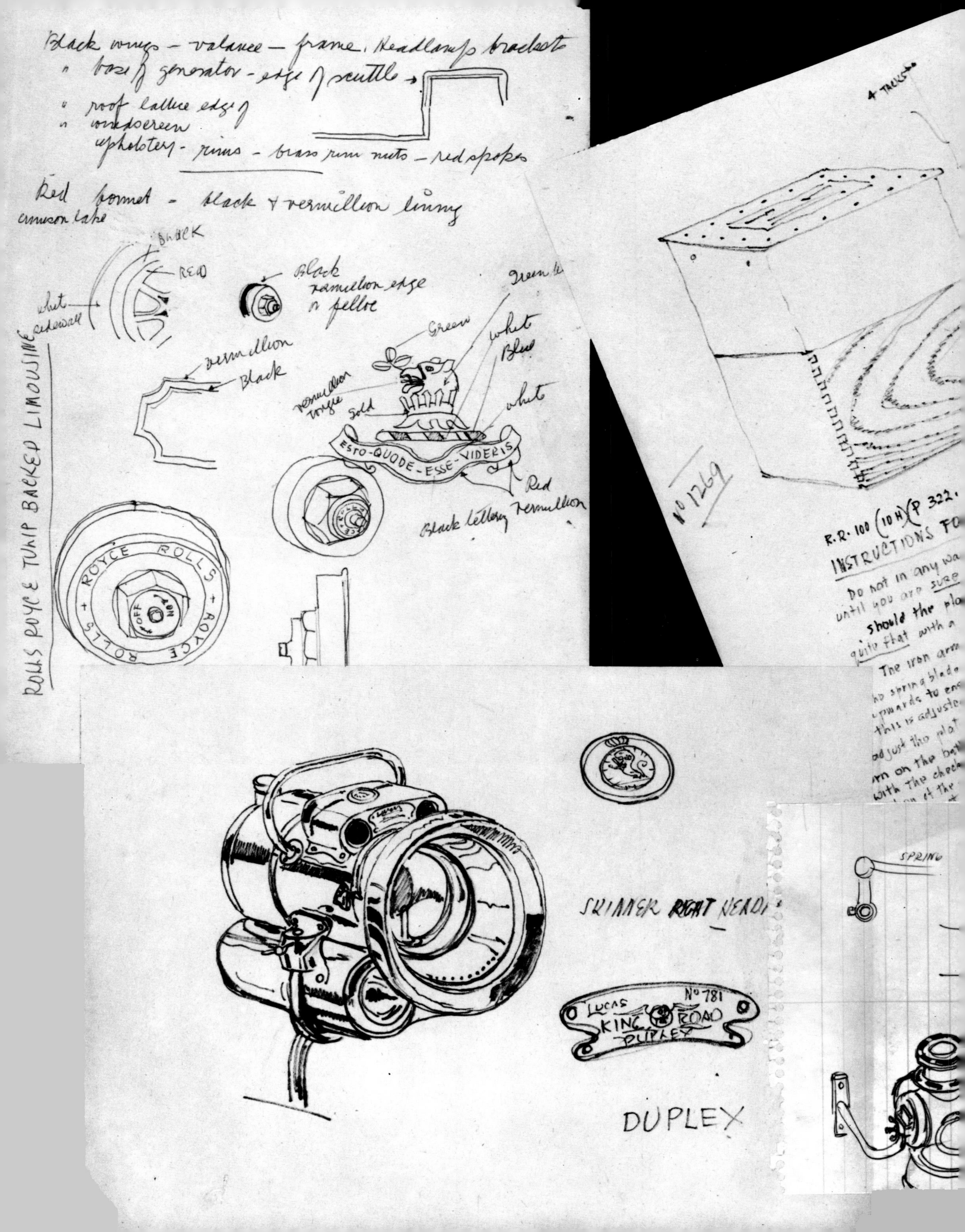

Black wings – valance – frame. Headlamp brackets
  „ base of generator – edge of scuttle →
  „ roof lattice edge of
  „ windscreen
      upholstery – rims – brass rim nuts – red spokes

Red bonnet – black & vermillion lining
crimson lake

BLACK
RED
whit sidewall

vermillion
Black

Black
vermillion edge
„ felloe

Green
whit
Blue
whit

Green le

vermillion tongue
Gold

ESTO·QUODE·ESSE·VIDERIS

Red
vermillion

Black lettering

ROYCE ROLLS
ROLLS ROYCE
ON OFF

ROLLS ROYCE TULIP BACKED LIMOUSINE

4 TACKS

No 1269

R·R·100 (10 H·P 322
INSTRUCTIONS FO
Do not in any wa
until you are sure
Should the pla
quite that with a
The iron arm
no spring blade
upwards to en
this is adjuste
adjust this plat
on on the bath
with the chee
on of the

SKINNER RIGHT HEAD

SPRING

Lucas No 781
KING ROAD
DUPLEX

DUPLEX

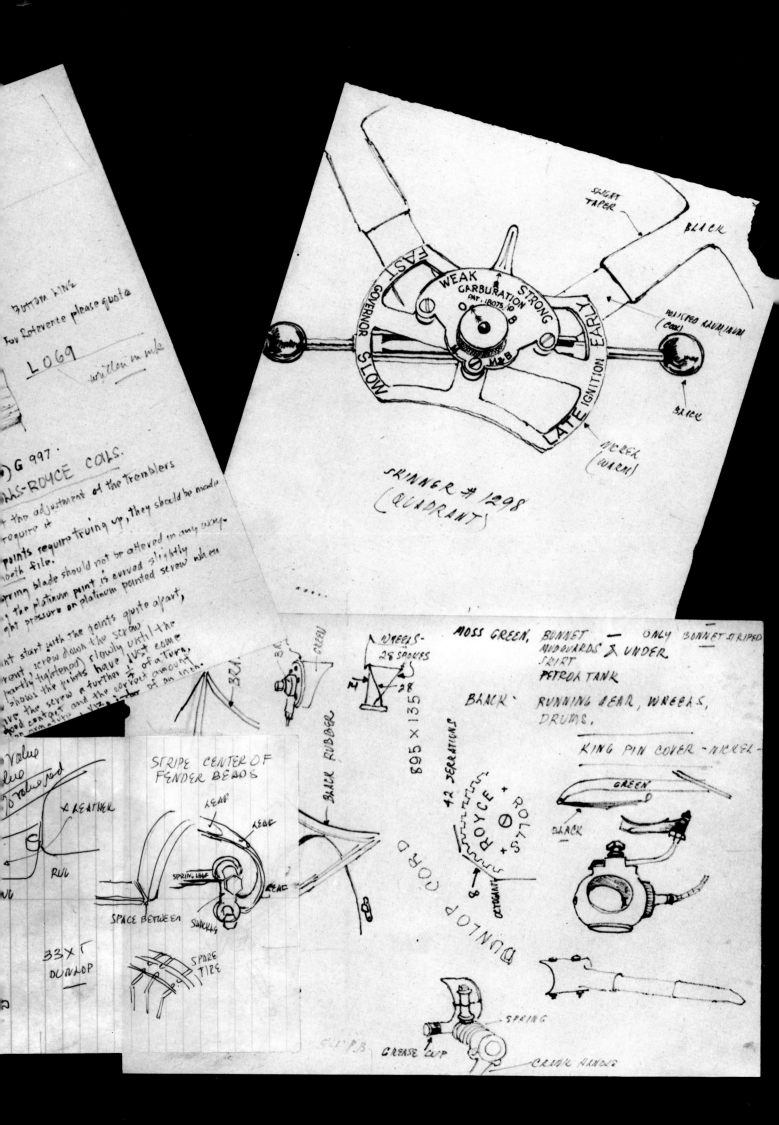

16 GRIPS BETWEEN SPOKES
(64 IN ALL)

3/4" RECESS TO COMB

BOTTOM OF RADIATOR 2"
BELOW FR

LAMP
8"
ACROSS

12" LONG

(Leake cat)

WHITE

BLUE

ASSOCIATE

ROYAL AUTOMOBILE CLUB ASSOCIATE
BRITISH AUTOMOBILE CLUB

N. 2780

forerunner of AA

MOTOR UNION

ALL
BRASS

1905

Stenson Cooky
Secretary

1909

BLACK
LETTERING

SMITH

30 males North
of Keighly

SERIF

DRIVING C
ISSUED B
AUTOMOBILE CLUB OF B

Owner's Driving Certificate.

This is to Certify that

Mr. William Slinger
of Goldilands,
Settle.

has been admitted to the Automobile Club
of Great Britain and Ireland, and that Ma

has a certificate to drive a

Small Power Patrol Car...

J. W. Orde
Secretary

Maudslay M
PARKSIDE

5"

4 1/2"

1"

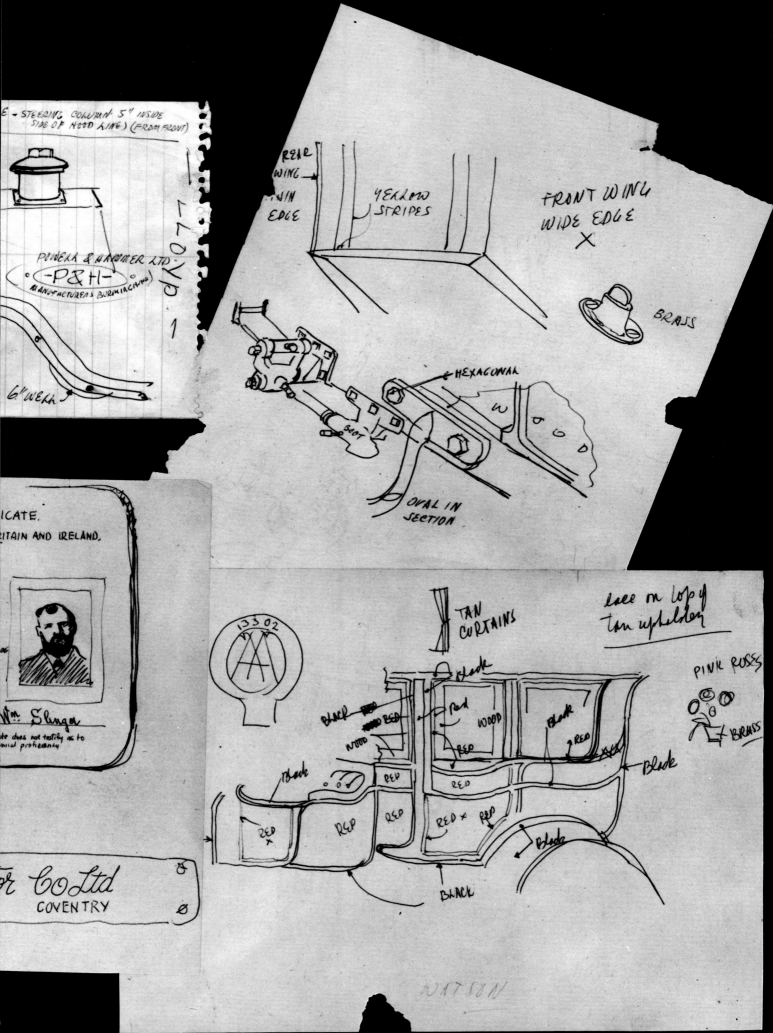

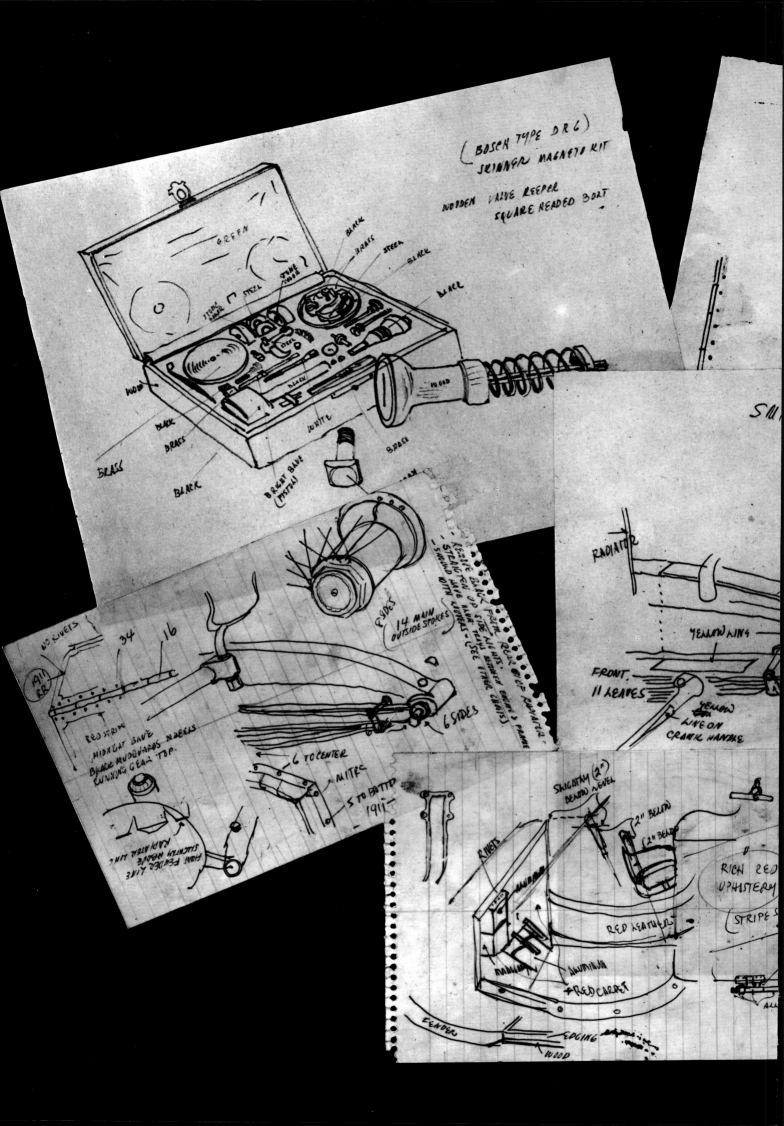

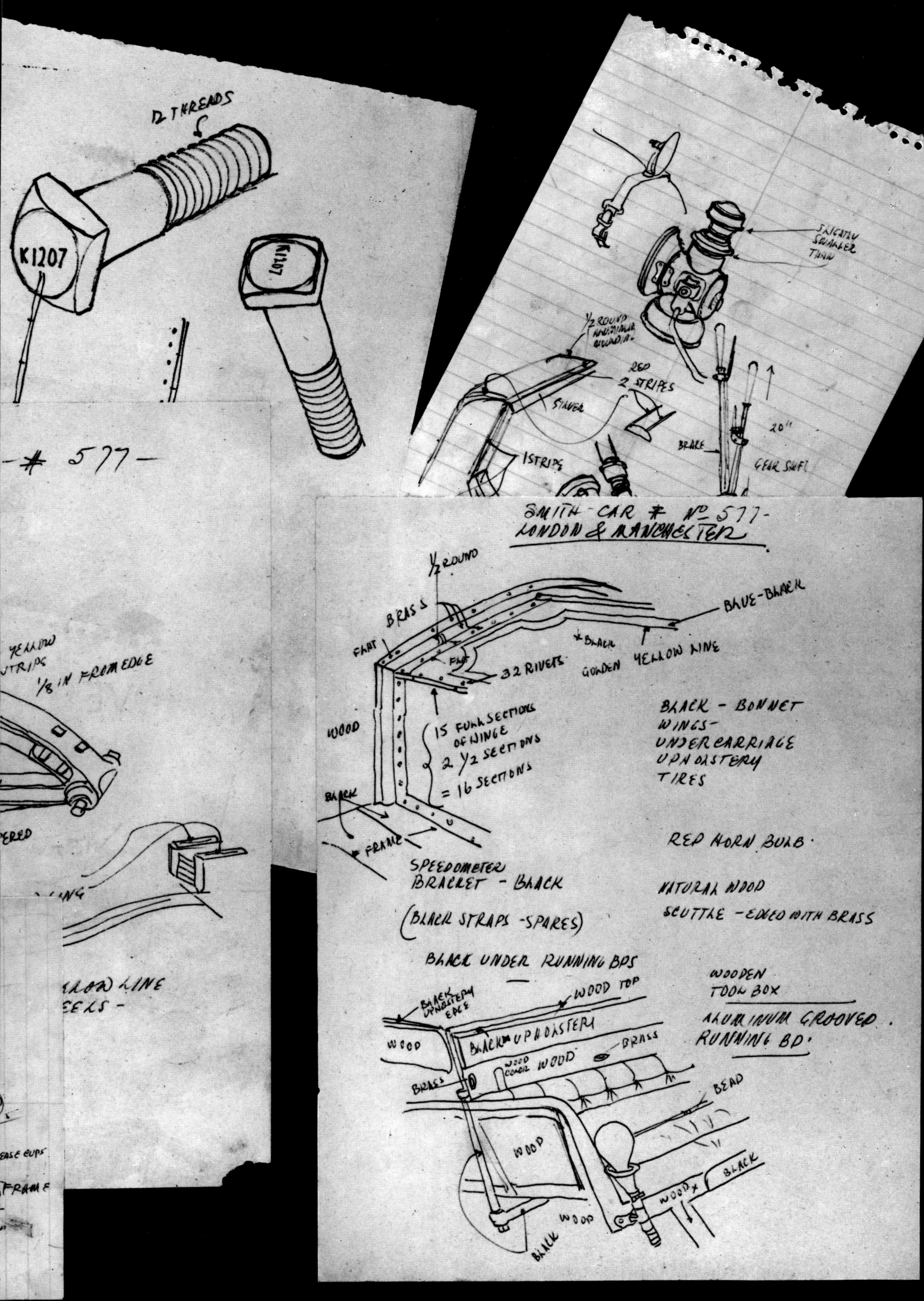

12 THREADS

K1207

K1207

577

SMITH CAR # N⁰ 577
LONDON & MANCHESTER

½ ROUND
BRASS
FLAT
FLAT
32 RIVETS
BLACK
GOLDEN YELLOW LINE
BLUE-BLACK

WOOD

15 FULL SECTIONS OF HINGE
2 ½ SECTIONS
= 16 SECTIONS

BLACK

FRAME

SPEEDOMETER
BRACKET - BLACK

(BLACK STRAPS - SPARES)

BLACK UNDER RUNNING BDS

BLACK - BONNET
WINGS -
UNDERCARRIAGE
UPHOLSTERY
TIRES

RED HORN BULB.

NATURAL WOOD
SCUTTLE - EDGED WITH BRASS

WOODEN
TOOL BOX

ALUMINUM GROOVED
RUNNING BD.

BLACK UPHOLSTERY EDGE
WOOD TOP
WOOD
BLACK UPHOLSTERY
BRASS
WOOD
WOOD COLOR WOOD
BRASS
BEAD
WOOD
BLACK
WOOD
WOOD
BLACK

SMOOTH SWALLER TANK

½ ROUND ALUMINUM BEAD A.

SILVER
RED
2 STRIPES
1 STRIPE
BRAKE
20"
GEAR SHFT

YELLOW STRIPE
⅛ IN FROM EDGE

ELLOW LINE
EELS -

EASE CUPS
FRAME

MEMORABILIA . . .

Artifacts, very often of a personal nature, are introduced throughout the gallery of paintings. Boyhood treasures, most of them brought to America by the painter in 1918,* are typical of the period, and are listed here for identification.

THE FIRST SILVER GHOST. Owned by Rolls-Royce, Ltd. It is shown in front of the Cook Street factory in Manchester in 1907. Enshrined in the "Rolls-Royce Family Album" in the glass case, paintings of Frederick Henry Royce and Charles Stewart Rolls from photographs supplied by Rolls-Royce, Ltd. Painting (top right) First Rolls-Royce sold to a private owner in England . . . a 10-horsepower, two-seater, two-cylinder car of 1904. From photographic clipping.
Painting (lower right) One of the first three Royce three-cylinder cars, from photograph supplied by Rolls-Royce, Ltd. Suspended by a thread over the bonnet of the car is the Koh-i-noor diamond, symbol of excellence. The painting on the brick wall is from an advertisement of the period. Page 25

SHOOTING BRAKE. Owned by Mr. James P. Smith, Keighley, Yorkshire, England. Gun and game bag courtesy of James Purdey & Sons, Ltd., London. License plate from companion Rolls-Royce to SU-76. Certificate of Merit from original in possession of Mr. James P. Smith, Keighley, Yorkshire, England. Badge Motor Union, forerunner of R.A.C. Badge, is worn on shooting brake. London and Manchester Plaque No. 577 is from Shooting Brake. *RR* enameled pin awarded to David Hart by Rolls-Royce, Ltd., in possession of Mr. James P. Smith. Scottish Automobile Club Badge. 12-gauge cartridges from James Purdey & Sons, Ltd. Maker's nameplate Maudslay Motor Co., Ltd., Parkside, Coventry, is from sill of shooting brake. Kildrummy Castle ruins . . . from postcard lent by Mr. James P. Smith. Page 32

PEARL OF THE EAST. (Not in existence) Imaginary scene somewhere in Ghats Mountains between Bombay and Kolhapur, India. The race scene in top lower left of painting is from a photograph showing C. S. Rolls winning the Tourist Trials Race, Isle of Man, 1906. Scene at lower left is from photograph of the Gardens of Shalimar in Lahore, India, built by Shah Jahan for Mumtaz Mahal, his wife. Page 36

QUEEN MARY'S ROLLS-ROYCE. (Not in existence) Imaginary scene in war-torn Belgium, World War I. Red Cross button issued in Australia in World War I, brought to America by the painter. Page 40

C. S. ROLLS' BALLOON CAR. (Not in existence) The English scene is imaginary. The balloon is meant to suggest that of Mr. Rolls, and is of the period. The rose and calling card resting on the well-clipped yew hedge are in tribute to Charles Stewart Rolls. The black-and-white painting is from a press release photograph of the period. Page 44

BARKER FLUSH-SIDE TORPEDO. Owned by Mr. S. J. Skinner, Basingstoke, Hants., England. Stars on blue field are part of the constellation Southern Cross on the Australian flag. The Union Jack is from one brought to America by the painter. It flew from one of the many triumphal arches erected in Melbourne by the painter's father on the occasion of the visit to Australia in 1901, on H.M.S. *Ophir*, of the Duke and Duchess of Cornwall and York, later King George V and Queen Mary. To portray a feeling of far-flung empire: yachtlike paddle steamer which plied Port Phillip Bay, the *Ozone*, one of three owned by Huddart-Parker of Melbourne . . . an imaginary castle mirrored in a placid sea . . . the Taj Mahal. The painter's Anzac medal, issued by the Department of Education, Victoria, Australia, in 1916 to commemorate the landing of Australian Imperial Forces at Anzac Cove in Gallipoli, April 25, 1915. A cigarette lighter made from a French 75 shell casing in France during World War I, given to painter years later in America. The Rolls-Royce mascot is from the painter's Phantom I. The red *RR* nameplate is from the painter's collection of Rolls-Royciana.

The Australian Military Badge is from a soldier's hat that saw service at Gallipoli, owned by painter. The brass button of Edward VII's Reign is from uniform tunic of painter's father. The penny and florin lying on the ermine robe belong to the painter. The chambered nautilus is considered by experts to be "the best shell in the world." Page 48

THE SELF-DRIVING PHAETON. (Not in existence) The English scene is imaginary. The monarch butterfly is a collector's favorite. The vintage Bosch magneto kit is owned by Mr. S. J. Skinner, Basingstoke, Hants, England. The old pipe, made by Peterson, Dublin, belonged to the painter's father. The Happy Thoughts tobacco tin held part of painter's collection of "treasures" including the florin, brought to America when a boy. Page 52

THE TULIP-BACKED LIMOUSINE. Owned by Mr. W. F. Watson, Bognor Regis, Sussex, England. An Edward VII penny near signature. Coat of Arms of Watson Family. The Edward VII Royal Automobile Club Badge as worn on the tulip-backed Limousine. Plaque No. 1543 is from the Watson car, as is the sill plate, J. A. Lawton & Co., London and Paris. The other Lawton brass plate is mounted on the scuttle of the tulip-backed Limousine. The setting for the painting was inspired by a visit to Stowe, Buckinghamshire, former seat of the Dukes of Buckingham during the period of the Hanoverian kings. Lace is of the period. Page 56

THE LONDON–EDINBURGH—1911. (Not in existence) Imaginary Scottish setting. The thistle brooch is from one lent by Mrs. Rowland Oakes, Bridgewater, Connecticut, formerly of Tiverton, Devonshire, England. Painting below is from literature of the period. The brass button is of World War I vintage. The lower right painting is from an early press release photograph and shows S.G. 551 during Scottish Reliability Trials of 1907. Page 60

PRIDE OF A MAHARAJAH—1911. Owned by Mr. James Leake, Muskogee, Oklahoma. The scene is composed; it is not factual. Plaque No. 1683 is from Mr. Leake's 1911 Silver Ghost Touring Victoria. Indian amulet lent by Mrs. Edward Wells, Bridgewater, Connecticut. Page 64

HOOPER LIMOUSINE—1911. Owned by Stanley E. Sears, Bolney, Sussex, England. Scene is imaginary but is based on a gateway the painter saw in England. The Edward VII Royal Automobile Club Badge is worn on Hooper limousine. The Hooper & Co., Ltd., brass plaque is based on Hooper & Co., Ltd., literature. The brass plaque No. 1721 is from the Hooper limousine. Penny of George V reign is from painter's collection. Page 68

LONDON–EDINBURGH TYPE—1913. (Not in existence) Scene inspired by grounds at Sharsted Court, home of Canon and Mrs. Eustace Wade and family, Newnham, near Sittingbourne, Kent, England. The texture of the brick and flint masonry behind car is interesting and typical of the region. Instrument detail painting "clipped" to side of painting is from interior of Barker flush-side torpedo, owned by Mr. S. J. Skinner, shown on page 51. Page 72

THE CONTINENTAL—Alpine Eagle—1913. Plaque No. 2260-E Owned by Mr. W. F. Watson, Bognor Regis, Sussex, England. Imaginary alpine scene. Detail from map of route of the 1913 Alpine Trials published in *The Autocar* of July, 1913. Painting from press release which appeared also in *The Autocar* showing No. 2260-E, first in at Riva. Page 76

THE YELLOW ROLLS-ROYCE—1914. (Not in existence) The English setting is imaginary. However, the beautiful inn sign is existent and can be found at Thame, Oxfordshire, England, in front of the Spread Eagle Inn. The painting of the 1906 driving certificate issued by the Automobile Club of Great Britain and Ireland is rare. It is owned by Mr. James P. Smith, Keighley, Yorkshire, England. The sill plate is imaginary, but Mann Egerton & Co., Ltd., Norwich and London, did the coachwork. The florin is from the painter's collection. Page 80

KING GEORGE'S ROLLS-ROYCE—1914. (Not in existence) Imaginary scene somewhere in Europe during World War I. In the background is the battleship *Queen Elizabeth*, the finest in the British Navy at the time. The Australian soldier's hat, cigarette lighter, and coins are listed elsewhere. The shoulder strap insignia *Australia*, the match box cover with the allied flags and the legend "These Colours Will Not Run," the Red Cross buttons, one honoring Nurse Edith Cavell, are part of the painter's collection. The postcard of the Pyramids was sent to the Brindle family by Roger Jones, a 17-year-old neighbor (who lied about his age to enlist) a week or so before landing at Anzac Cove, where he was killed. The *Lusitania*, torpedoed in 1915, the news of which is still vividly remembered. The button lying on the cobblestones was given to the painter by a French bombardier who was traveling on S.S. *Sonoma* to America with the Brindle family in November–December, 1918. Page 84

DOWAGER EMPRESS MARIE'S ROLLS-ROYCE. (Not in existence) Façade of Ekaterininsky Palace near St. Petersburg. Royal Coat of Arms of the Russian royal family—the two-headed eagle. In gold frame, breast decoration with miniature of Peter I. Page 88

FIVE-SEATER, TWO-DOOR TOURING CAR—1914. (Not in existence) The background for this painting was inspired by a visit to Stowe, Buckinghamshire, England, seat of the Dukes of Buckingham during the reign of the Hanoverian kings. The shape of the arch and the classic radiator speak for themselves. Page 92

PRINCE YUSUPOV'S ROLLS-ROYCE—1914. (Not in existence) This winter scene shows the Neva river and St. Petersburg in the background, the footprints in the snow leading to the river. Glass of poisoned Madeira, portrait of Rasputin and quote from Yusupov's book, *La Fin de Rasputin*, 1919. Page 96

1914 SKIFF IN EGYPT. Owned by Dr. R. O. Barnard, Chiddingfold, Surrey, England. The Egyptian scene is imaginary. The framed painting is from photograph taken by painter in Mrs. Barnard's English garden. Part of her collection of erica (heather) shows in foreground. Dagger and sheath painted from artifacts taken from Tutankhamen's Tomb. Car's chassis number is 54 PB. Page 100

ROLLS-ROYCE ARMORED CAR—1914. (Not in existence) Clipped to painting at left is black-and-white painting of T. E. Lawrence from press photograph. Quote "A Rolls in the desert is worth more than rubies" is from Lawrence's book *Seven Pillars of Wisdom*. Painting of Lawrence astride motorcycle on which he was killed near Dorset, May 13, 1935. Dynamite brick of the type used by Lawrence. Anzac medal dated 1918 owned by painter. Page 104

---

* Surely I must have had a premonition of just how invaluable they would be to me fifty years later!